€ 5.00

€ 5.00

The book of
BIRDS

A. M. LYSAGHT

The book of
BIRDS

*Five centuries
of bird illustration*

CHANCELLOR
PRESS

First published in Great Britain in 1975 by
Phaidon Press Ltd

This edition published in 1984 by
Chancellor Press
59 Grosvenor Street
London W1

© 1975 A. M. Lysaght

ISBN 0 907486 60 6

Printed in Hong Kong

Contents

For Justin

Acknowledgements

MANY PEOPLE have helped me with the preparation of this book; I deeply regret that it is impossible to thank them all individually since the material has been drawn from a wide variety of sources.

The printed books on which I have chiefly relied for background information are the following: *The Folklore of Birds* (1958) by E. A. Armstrong; both editions of *A Dictionary of Birds* (1893–6, ed. Alfred Newton *et al*; 1964, ed. A. Landsborough Thomson); *Bird Books and Bird Art* (1938) by Jean Anker; and the numerous publications on zoological illustration by Dr Claus Nissen who kindly allowed me access to the proofs of his current index (in the press) of the artists mentioned in his various writings. I also made extensive use of George Sarton's *Introduction to the History of Science* (1931–47).

His Grace the Duke of Northumberland generously allowed me to examine the Sherborne Missal, and to reproduce two details from it (Plates 7, 8).

The books and other manuscripts from which illustrations and other material have been taken belong to the following libraries and institutions:

> The British Library; the British Museum; the British Museum (Natural History); the Pepysian Library, Magdalene College, Cambridge; the Balfour Library, Department of Zoology, University of Cambridge; the Lindley Library, Royal Horticultural Society, London; the India Office Library; the library of the Zoological Society of London; the Royal Academy of Arts; the Royal College of Art; the Linnean Society; and the Library of the Department of the History of Science and Technology, Imperial College of Science and Technology.

I am most grateful to the trustees and directors of these institutions (and in the case of the Pepysian Library, to the Masters and Fellows, Magdalene College, Cambridge) for permission to use their material, and to the librarians for help of many kinds. I am particularly indebted to the Librarian and to Mrs Ann Datta of the British Museum (Natural History) on whose time and patience I have made many demands. Mr Gavin Bridson of the Linnean Society, who has a lifelong interest in animal illustration, has given me all sorts of assistance and has discussed much of this book in the course of its preparation. Mr Dennis Paisey of the British Library drew my attention to the hitherto unknown sixteenth-century German broadsheet of a ruff (Plates 31, 32); Dr Dennis Rhodes, incunabulist of the same library, gave me help in his own field. In the British Museum members of the Department of Oriental Antiquities and Oriental Manuscripts, the Print Room and the Manuscript Room, all guided me to some of their great treasures, a few of which have been selected for reproduction here. Mr Derek Goodwin of the British Museum (Natural History) kindly checked many of my ornithological notes but all mistakes are entirely my own responsibility. Thanks are also due to Dr Joseph Needham and Mr Peter Hammond who kindly advised me on source publications concerned with Chinese bird lore and avian drugs. Professor E. H. Warmington generously extricated me from a maze of misunderstanding involving the zoological section of the *Dioscorides Codex*. The directors of Messrs Bernard Quaritch Ltd, London (Antiquarian Booksellers) allowed me to reproduce some rare items from their valuable collection (Plates 23, 49, 106–109, 123). Plates 55, 103 and 127 were reproduced from books in the possession of David Evans (Fine Bird Books), Pitt, Winchester. Mr E. Hughes of the Balfour Library gave me special assistance with the paintings of Webb-Smith.

I owe a special debt to Mrs Roslyn Poignant and Dr Norman A. F. Smith who read and criticized the introduction in manuscript, and advised me on anthropological and historical matters. Finally it is my pleasure to thank Mr A. Whitworth and his staff of the Lyon Playfair Library, Imperial College of Science and Technology, for the many kind facilities I have enjoyed while writing this book.

Most of the illustrations in this book were photographed at the British Museum (Natural History). In addition to these, and the few mentioned above, the plates belonging to the libraries listed here are the following:

British Library 4, 11–14, 16–18, 22, 31, 32, 36–45, 68, 96
British Museum 1, 6, 9, 10, 19–21, 63, 65, 66, 74, 142
Balfour Library 125, 126, 132, 133
India Office Library 59, 122
Lindley Library 35, 46
Linnean Society 57, 58
Pepysian Library 15
Phaidon Press Ltd 5
Royal Academy of Arts 86
Royal College of Art 118, 119
Zoological Society 102, 111, 124, 134, 140

Introduction

THE ART OF BIRD ILLUSTRATION is extremely old. Some of the incised and painted representations by palaeolithic man still retain their power to move us; they are in many cases so skilful that it is plain that they were based on an older and more ephemeral art of remote antiquity, probably originating as drawings in mud or sand.

The history of bird illustration carries us back to the magico-religious myths of the earliest civilizations; certain birds connected with these myths appear over and over again in paintings, mosaics and embroideries. Much sympathetic magic and primitive medical practice was based on the mysterious powers with which birds were supposed to be endowed, and this made it essential to identify and distinguish between them. The earliest comprehensive system of which we have definite knowledge was promulgated by Aristotle who is generally regarded as the father of scientific zoology as we know it today. There must, however, have been a considerable corpus of earlier knowledge on which he could draw, and it is probable that primitive schemes of classification were developed by the ancient Egyptians and Sumerians.

In the following pages some of the observations of birds that have stimulated men to delineate them will be briefly outlined and we shall try to see how the knowledge of birds was developed by their use in medicine, by the ancient sport of falconry, by the homing ability of some birds such as pigeons, which were then trained as messengers. We shall see how the ancient Egyptians painted birds with a skill and precision that was later lost for more than two thousand years, and how methods and techniques similar to theirs arose independently in western Europe in the Middle Ages and led ultimately to the magnificent paintings in the scientific books of the late eighteenth and early nineteenth centuries. We shall see, too, how the Chinese, equally skilful, reached a high standard of aesthetic accomplishment in the tenth century, perhaps earlier, but their interest in birds was largely confined to their use in medicine, or as decorative symbols, and this retarded the development of scientific ornithology in their country. It may be for similar reasons that highly gifted Indian painters, such as Ustad Mansur, of the seventeenth and eighteenth centuries, seem to be rather isolated figures. All of this suggests that scientific ornithology was above all a western European development, but that there was a shared background of myth and magic; we can only understand what has occurred in the last four centuries by examining the main facets, although necessarily in a superficial manner, of the historic background.

Man's capacity for aesthetic enjoyment may have been the most useful of his characteristics, for it was one of the most powerful of the impulses that led him to investigate the nature of the world about him. Perhaps the earliest recognition of this came to one of our prehistoric ancestors, lying on a cliff top and watching to see where the birds were nesting. As he planned how best to rob them of their eggs or young, he may have noticed how they soared and glided in the up-currents, caused by the winds beating against the cliff face, and how some of these birds—especially the ravens and falcons—performed elaborate aerobatics apparently unrelated to the collection of food or the guarding of their nests. Perhaps he noticed too the marvellous synchronization of wheeling flocks of migrant birds, and wondered at it, as we still do today when, with all our scientific equipment, we seem no nearer to an explanation of how it happens.

It is probable, however, that man's initial stimulus for observing birds precisely arose from their value as food; this would have led our ancestors in temperate climates to associate spring with the arrival of migrants and an abundant egg supply, and winter, with their replacement by non-breeding Arctic species so that in the coldest, darkest days there were at least supplies of ducks and geese for skilled hunters.

From the fowlers' observations would have arisen the desire to use the most dashing birds of prey for capturing other birds. The almost world-wide distribution of the peregrine falcon, the female of which is the best hunter of all birds, may have led to the development of hawking in several different parts of the world. The earliest record discovered so far appears to be an Assyrian sculpture in Khorsabad, about 1200 BC, showing a falconer with a hawk on his wrist.

The taming of pigeons and their training as messengers is probably very ancient also. It is likely that the Chinese and the Sumerians practised this as well as the ancient Egyptians. These last people included pigeons amongst the birds with which they decorated their tombs. One such painting, for instance, is to be seen on the coffin of Djehuty-Nekht, a local prince buried at Bersheh some eighteen hundred years before the birth of Christ. It is a remarkably accurate, opalescent rendering of a pigeon by an unknown artist who used a technique similar to that of the French Impressionists. Pigeons were widely used by the Greeks and Romans as messengers and have continued to be so employed until the present day. During the siege of Paris in the Franco-Prussian war 150,000 official messages and an even larger number of private ones were carried by pigeons (the Prussians loosed hawks against them). In the Second World War they were valued for bearing messages to Resistance groups in Europe, and taking SOS calls from ditched aircraft. A constant supply of birds with highly developed navigational ability is ensured through the sport of pigeon racing which has a very large number of adherents in England alone, but pigeons are not the only birds to be used as messengers; in Polynesia frigate-birds have been similarly employed to take communications from one island to another.

Man's use of birds, combined with his awe at their ability to fly, their seasonal wanderings, their skill in nest-building, the beauty of their song and the splendour of breeding plumage in many species, inspired the sense of magic and mystery which man expressed in myths, in ritual dances and in his paintings. In many societies man believed that he could increase his prowess by eating selected parts of birds; just as in some countries it was thought that warriors gained valour by devouring the heart or brain of a courageous man slain in battle. Related to this is the use of avian drugs in early medicine.

For these reasons it became desirable to be able to identify birds precisely; the Egyptians and the Chinese, in different ways, appear to have been the first to systematize this knowledge; it is probable that as the archaeologists of today uncover more and more of our early history we shall gain greater insight into the initial approaches to scientific ornithology.

For the identification of birds, drawings and diagrams were better than descriptions. Until books were invented, oral descriptions had to serve; it is important to remember that oral records were in many cases remarkably precise, and that a great deal of esoteric lore was handed down before any kind of script came into use.

The earliest surviving graphic records were the drawings and paintings made by primitive man in caves and on sheltered rock faces in many parts of the world. The power of those to be seen in the caves of Lascaux in the Dordogne, is as much a result of the artist's concentration as of the religious purpose that motivated him. We do not know the meaning of the bird in the scene of the man killed by a rhinoceros, which is obviously a stylized representation.

Other prehistoric paintings or incised drawings in the caves of southern Spain, northern Africa and South America represent species that can be identified with certainty today, and show that the artists had acute powers of observation and considerable technical skill. These drawings are not merely representations of dead birds in conventional static positions; they sometimes show them in flight, or displaying as in the case of a Great Bustard in a cave in southern Andalusia.

Thus bird cults seem to have flourished in palaeolithic times; among other things birds may have represented the soul just as the dove is still the symbol of the Holy Ghost in Christian communities. After prehistoric times we find birds on poles incised on Hittite seals, and similar emblems passed via Scythian art to India. There was a tendency in later ages for birds to be represented as human beings with avian characters, or as birds with the features of mammals other than man. Thus we have the lion-headed eagle of the Sumerians, and their bird-footed winged goddess, Lilith, rather more than two thousand years before Christ. Eagle masks were used in rituals as we know from an Assyrian frieze at Nimrud about a thousand years later; the eagle was the emblem of the god Ashur. Coming down through the ages to this century it was still possible, twenty years ago, to find local carvings of sinister bird men in Bali.

In the last hundred years many scholars have worked on the history of myths, which may be worth considering in some detail, as they have persisted through the ages in many surprising ways.

There is a considerable body of evidence relating to goose myths which are very widespread. These birds may have been among the first animals to be domesticated owing to the fact that the newly hatched young become fixated or imprinted on the first large moving creature that they see. Thus they may suddenly develop a passionate attachment to beings as different from their own parents as a man, a pig or a poodle. This could perhaps explain the source of Titania's passion for Bottom.

Goose bones were used as oracles in ancient times to determine the most favourable moment for waging war, and some trace of the veneration in which they were then held still lingers in our current belief that a lucky break in a wishbone will make our wishes come true. A goose and a goat led the Christian forces in the First Crusade of 1096. Long before this the Chinese killed geese to celebrate the summer solstice, but in Korea a similar feast was held in midwinter. England traditionally feasts on geese at Michaelmas on 29 September, but most Europeans do so at Martinmas which is on 11 November. The goose is also associated with the Greek goddess Aphrodite, who has many affinities with eastern avian myths; it was one of her sacred birds. In China it is still traditional in some districts for the family of the bridegroom to offer live geese to the bride; while, in Turkey, erotic cults connected with geese are still extant.

One of the most interesting of all the myths relating to these birds is the belief that some kinds were not hatched from eggs but sprang from trees. The best known of these myths is that of the Barnacle Goose (see Plates 28 and 29), which was fully worked out earlier this century by Heron-Allen. This myth was very widely diffused. There is an ancient Chinese fable that a small and brilliantly coloured bird did not hatch in the ordinary way but grew out of the flower above which it was seen hovering. This sounds like a humming-bird but these do not occur in China, so the myth may have originated in North America and have spread from the Rockies, where these birds are common, across Bering Strait to the Far East. The Barnacle Goose myth seems quite definitely to have been current in Minoan times. Mycenaean pottery shows us a number of designs in which geese are connected with the ship's barnacle. The shell of this barnacle is very different from that of its relatives, the crab and the shrimp; its feathery appendages and its abundant presence on ships' timbers as well as on drift-wood which gathers on many shores where small sea birds are stranded by winter storms, seem to have given rise to the idea (which gained currency in the Middle Ages) that geese sprang from the barnacles hanging from a tree bending over water, and that they were more of the nature of fish than of fowl. The myth was actively promoted by members of the Church since, if the birds were not engendered in the ordinary way, they were not truly flesh and could therefore be eaten in Lent and on other fast days. In the eleventh century, a cardinal bishop of Ostia, Pietro Damiani, authoritatively pronounced that birds could be produced by trees. Albertus Magnus denied it, so did Neckham. 'Rumour has it', said he, 'that by a process of Nature pinewood steeped in the sea gives forth young birds. This is done by a vitreous humour: what public opinion asserts, philosophy indignantly denies.' In 1187 Giraldus Cambrensis found the myth current in Ireland where indeed, in some remote parts, it had adherents this century. It was so widespread in Europe that it found its way into some of the early printed books.

The two illustrations of the myth in this volume are a woodcut by L'Obel (commemorated in *Lobelia*) showing a tree hung with barnacles, and the geese that bred from it. It was reprinted by Plantin in Antwerp, and in a slightly more elaborate version by Aldrovandi, who had his doubts about the whole matter, but stated that since the belief was maintained by so many people he supposed that it might be true. The writer who made the most of the legend in England was Gerard, compiler of the famous *Herball* of 1597 which, in spite of being largely an inaccurate crib from Dodoens, is on the whole a valuable survey of botanical knowledge at the end of the sixteenth century. The *Herball* ends with his account of the Barnacle or Tree Goose as it used to be called:

> There is [he wrote] a small island in Lancashire called the Pile of Foulders (on the west side of the entrance to Morecambe Bay, about fifteen miles south of Ulverston) wherein are found the broken pieces of old and bruised ships, and also the trunks and bodies, with the branches of old and rotten trees, cast up there likewise; whereon is found a certain spume, or froth, that in time breedeth into certain shells, in shape like those of a muskle, but sharper pointed, and of a whitish colour, wherein is contained a thing in form like a lace of silk, finely woven as it were together; one end whereof is fastened unto the inside of the shell, even as the fish of oisters and muskles are; the other end is made fast unto the belly of a rude masses or lump, which in time cometh to the shape and form of a bird: when it is perfectly formed, the shell gapeth open, and the first thing that appeareth is the aforesaid lace or string; next come the legs of the bird hanging out, and as it groweth greater, it openeth the shell by degrees, till at length it is all come forth, and hangeth only by the bill; in short space after it cometh to full maturitie, and falleth into the sea, where it gathereth feathers, and groweth to a fowl bigger than a Mallard and lesser than a Goose, which the people in Lancashire call by no other name than a Tree-Goose: which place aforesaid, and all those parts adjoining, do so much abound therewith, that one of the best is bought for threepence.

Gerard was so convinced of the truth of what he wrote that he ended: 'If any doubt, may it please them to repair to me, and I shall satisfie them by the testimonie of good witnesses.'

Goose myths are amongst the best known but myths concerning other birds recur over and over again. Ravens and owls are of particular interest because of man's ambivalent tendency to fear as well as cherish creatures that appear to have supernatural powers. Ravens and magpies, for instance, may bring good or bad luck according to the number seen. Most of us know the old jingle about the magpie:

> *One for sorrow, two for joy,*
> *Three for a girl, four for a boy.*

Ravens gathering over corpses on a battlefield led to the belief that they were able to predict death. The fact that they have been seen to peck out the eyes of the dead gave rise to the idea that they possess exceptional sight. There is also a Welsh tradition that blind people who are kind to ravens may be cured, and another in Czechoslovakia that a man may become a good shot by eating the charred hearts of three ravens.

In the Babylonian account of the flood (from which that in Genesis is derived), the dove, the swallow and the raven went from the ark to find out whether the waters had subsided. We find that this role of the raven as a messenger is widespread. Odin had two tame ravens who flew abroad daily, encircling the world to gather news which they whispered in his ear as they perched on his shoulder. In the Hebrides a boy was thought to gain special insight, which enabled him to locate the dead, by drinking from a raven's skull. The ravens that live in the Tower of London are believed to be essential to the good of the realm; it is said that if they vanish Britain will perish. There is a widespread association between ravens and the weather, possibly due to the fact that soaring ravens are conspicuous in the strong up-currents that are a feature of thundery weather.

Owls are more often regarded as birds of doom than of good omen. Their nocturnal habits and their cries, so often hoots or shrieks, their silent flight and their enormous eyes have fascinated mankind for as long as records have existed. In parts of India it is believed that dissolute men turn into owls at death. If one of these birds alights on a house on a certain night of the week special rites must be enacted to avert misfortune: the owner of the house must tie a dark woollen thread below the cross beam and a naked person must add as many knots as there were screeches. Threads are still hung in some Hebridean houses to wipe out misfortune, more especially to avert evil after the disturbance of ancient burial grounds. In some areas of Transylvania farmers walk naked round their fields to keep the birds away.

The remarkable vision possessed by owls has led to various practices based on sympathetic magic. In parts of India the eyeballs of an owl are eaten in the hope of improving sight. In the United States Cherokee Indians bathed children's eyes in water containing owl feathers in order to keep them awake at night. In Yorkshire a broth made from owls is considered good for whooping cough; the owl hoots when it is in good health so that a potion made from it is bound to cure the whooping child. A very ancient belief, that owls' eggs were a cure for dipsomania, dates back to Philostratus and persisted in England until the seventeenth century. This originated from the legends about Athene, the goddess who sprang from the head of Zeus; the owl was her symbol and therefore appears as the embodiment of wisdom in pictures and engravings throughout the ages.

All the attributes of Athene were opposed to those of Dionysus, a god who appears to have been introduced into Greece by an Asian people about 800 BC, and who symbolized licence and ecstasy in all its forms. This is connected with a German belief that the heart and right foot of an owl carried in the left armpit provide immunity from the bites of a mad dog. According to Pliny, an owl's heart placed on the breast of a sleeping woman will cause her to divulge her secrets. In China the owl is supposed to keep thunder away and in Germany it was believed to have the same effect on hail and lightning.

This widespread use of the owl as a symbol of both good and evil has led to its being portrayed in a diversity of ways both in prehistoric sculpture and in the graphic arts of most countries. Today it has lost none of its interest and drawings of owls are among the most popular of all representations of birds.

Another favourite subject amongst artists throughout the ages is the eagle which has given rise to a very extensive body of myth. Owing to the belief that it was able to look at the sun without damage to its eyes, and also that it flew to greater heights than most other birds, it assumed heraldic significance. In the third millennium BC it was associated with the concept of light in Sumerian cultures, as well as with the gods of fertility and war. The Hittites adopted the eagle as an emblem, and were followed by the Greeks (the presence of an eagle above the cliffs of Delphi is still regarded as oracular), then by the Romans, for whom the bird was a military symbol of the greatest significance, and finally by some great European countries, the United States and Australia.

The size of eagles probably gave rise to the legends of the Rukh of India, the forebear of the Roc of the Arabian Nights. Garuda, another giant Indian bird of prey and the vehicle of Vishnu, was a part of this tradition, as was also the vast Simurgh of the Persians, and the Phang, the storm-bird of China. In Siberia the Chukchees believe in the Noga-bird which is large enough to attack elks and whales.

Eagles were often represented in conflict with snakes, symbolizing the age-old strife between the forces of good and evil—a world-wide myth which exists even in countries such as New Zealand where there are no snakes, though perhaps their place is taken by the very large landlocked eels that occur there.

At the opposite end of the scale from eagles is the wren, which is sometimes credited with outwitting the king of birds; thus it was believed that eating its roasted flesh sharpened a man's wits. In parts of the British Isles a wren hunt takes place on Boxing Day, the significance of which seems to lie in the identification of the crevice-loving wren with the powers of darkness, and their defeat by the powers of light and life as shown by the lengthening days of the New Year. Although the aim of the hunt was the slaughter of the bird, there was an opposing belief that it was unlucky to be associated with its death and a person destroying the nest might lose the use of his fingers.

From these few examples it is easy to understand how the extensive web of magico-religious beliefs eventually gave rise to medical practices and to the use of avian drugs that grew to have a traditional place in the treatment of diseases.

In his book *Chinese Materia Medica* (1932), Bernard Read has pointed out that the ancient civilizations used remarkably similar avian drugs. The sixteen species of birds from which drugs were derived by the early Chinese were also utilized by the Egyptians, the Syrians, the Arabs, the Persians, the Greeks and the Romans. One of the earliest documents concerned with this ancient lore is a part of the Egyptian *Papyrus Ebers* dating from the first half of the sixteenth century BC (the actual content is much older). This contains classified prescriptions for diseases of the eyes, skin, circulatory system, and reproductive organs, as well as a surgical section. Amongst the avian drugs known to have been used were the dried liver of a swallow, mixed with a fermenting drink, for treating a woman after an abortion and the excrement of a pelican in ophthalmology; similarly the blood of bats and lizards was regarded as valuable for certain conditions of the eye, and these animals are frequently represented in early English manuscripts.

The earliest Chinese ornithological text appears to be the *Ch'in Ching*, a title now given to a work of the Sung dynasty, but believed to be based on a much older text probably written before the Han dynasty, that is earlier than 200 BC. The Chinese regarded cranes as the symbol of longevity, and believed that after the age of sixteen hundred years they became immortal, a myth which, as we shall see later, is somewhat parallel to that of the Arabian phoenix. In Europe in medieval times cranes were served traditionally at banquets to promote longevity and they frequently figure in illuminated manuscripts.

Amongst other Chinese practices were the use of storks' eggs in the treatment of smallpox, the flesh of the mallard as a digestive and a vermifuge and the charred feathers and faeces of the white egret as an antidote to the bites of poisonous fishes and insects. The excrement of the cormorant mixed with lard was used in the treatment of red noses resulting from too much wine. For our purposes the importance of these treatments (some of which are so widespread that they may still deserve investigation) lies in the fact that long ago there was an imperative need for some sort of classification so that poisonous or useful plants and animals could be identified. The ancient Chinese had a very general way of classifying birds, but there does not appear to have been anything like a comprehensive system until the time of Aristotle.

Our knowledge of the three thousand years before Aristotle is fragmentary although records were kept for most of this time. The clay tablets of Babylonia and Assyria, which were literary as well as documentary in content, may be regarded as books; they were collected into libraries which were the pride of their owners and famous throughout the civilized world. The Assyrians employed tablets of soft clay on which their script, first pictographic and then cuneiform, was inscribed with a stylus. Each volume consisted of a series of numbered tablets stamped with the title of the work and the name of the library to which it belonged. They were then fired and became so hard that many have survived until the present day.

About 2600 BC the whole Mesopotamian valley was united to form Babylonia, one of whose most famous kings was Hammurabi, the law-giver. He built up a very fine library which included medical books. The Babylonians were succeeded by the Assyrians whose best-known library was formed by Ashurbanipal who established it finally in Nineveh. He owned a herbal of considerable length. When the barbarians finally destroyed that city they used battering rams to break down the city walls, which fell in such a way that they preserved many of the tablets which remained there until they were excavated by the archaeologists of the last two centuries.

In China written records go back to at least eleven centuries BC. The earliest were inscribed on bone but later silk was sized and used extensively. In 1973 and 1974, during excavations in Hunan, a silk shroud was found in the tomb of a lady of T'ai, of about 150 BC. This was splendidly painted with animals including owls and fabulous birds.

Egyptian records were sometimes inscribed on tablets similar to those employed by the Sumerians but more often they were written on papyrus. Layers of the pith from the reed were superimposed on each other at right angles and wetted and beaten. The resulting material was treated in various ways according to the uses to which it was to be put. Records were also kept on leather. Unfortunately all these materials were perishable and although there is evidence that there were both temple and palace libraries, all that we know about them is derived from fragments of papyrus, from wall paintings and from inscriptions in tombs. These last have shown us that as early as 3000 BC there were specially trained scribes who had titles such as 'Controller of the Library' and 'Keeper of the Scrolls' and were obviously regarded as notables.

In Egypt birds had great importance as religious and political symbols and although few of the early records have survived it is apparent from the wall paintings that the artists were highly skilled. One of the most famous friezes of antiquity is the painting of geese in the tomb of Ne-fer-Maat at Medum, executed about 3000 BC. These are all very precisely drawn and depict three species still flourishing today. In other tombs there are representations of falcons, ibises, waders, ducks and pigeons. There are many stone carvings of birds that were directly connected with the gods; thus a hawk was the symbol for Horus, the god of the sky, the sun and the moon; the ibis was the symbol for Thoth, the god of the scribes, that is of learning and intelligence, aptly chosen on account of his long bill with which he was always turning things over. The most important Egyptian painting in the context of the present book is a papyrus fragment from the first century BC now in the Berlin Museum. It consists of a series of drawings executed on a ruled and squared surface. One of these drawings shows a vulture from the back, and it is quite clear that we have here the earliest example of a model book, such as artists have always used, to record formulae for dealing with difficult poses. The very high quality of the early murals in the Egyptian tombs would seem to indicate that similar model books were in use thousands of years before this isolated example now in Berlin. It also seems probable that both the Egyptians and the Assyrians had some knowledge of the classification of birds, as well as of their structure and function.

The first known classification of birds and other animals that can be regarded as at all comprehensive was drawn up by Aristotle. His notes on birds, and those of his contemporaries and successors, were summarized in the last century by D'Arcy Thompson, who included references to a wide range of scholarly papers in his *Glossary of Greek Birds* (1895). Much of Aristotle's knowledge must have been available to the Athenians of his day since there were public libraries by then, and, indeed, more than one thousand years before he was born there was a literate civilization in Greece and Crete.

There seems little doubt that Aristotle himself owned one of the largest private libraries of the day. After his death part of it is supposed to have gone to the magnificent library at Alexandria which flourished until about 47 BC when much of it was burnt during Julius Caesar's conquest of Egypt. Mark Anthony is said to have given Cleopatra some 200,000 rolls from the library at Pergamum to replace those destroyed by Caesar. There was great rivalry between these two famous libraries. King Eumenes II of Pergamum (197–159 BC), who brought the library of his capital to its greatest perfection, used to try to persuade the Alexandrian scholars to join his staff, while the Egyptians on their side are said to have cut the supplies of papyrus to Pergamum to check the production of books there. It was then that the Pergamum librarians developed the use of a fine parchment (from the Latin *pergamena*) as a writing material which was more durable than papyrus. Leather had been in use for many centuries but parchment was much finer, more pliable and more easily cut so that books could be made in the form to which we are accustomed today.

It was perhaps from the Egyptians that the Minoans and then the Greeks learnt to paint birds with the great skill that is apparent in the surviving examples of their art. One of the liveliest Greek paintings shows Herakles and the Stymphalian birds in various attitudes of flight; it ornaments an Athenian vase of about 600 BC, now in the British Museum. Many such accomplished paintings must have been executed on papyrus and have perished, but Byzantine mosaics such as those at Aquileia, together with the vase paintings and murals, give an impression of acute observation and great skill on the part of the artists.

One manuscript with bird paintings has survived from AD 512. This is a copy of the *Dioscorides Codex*, an encyclopedia of *materia medica*, prepared by Dioscorides who flourished in the reigns of Claudius and Nero in the middle of the first century AD. It contains six hundred paintings of plants copied from a work by Krateuas (*c*.120–63 BC). The surviving copy in Vienna is written in Greek on vellum and contains a final section with paintings of forty-eight birds, many of which are named; there are notes on how to trap them, and some observations on their habits. In the fifteenth century a copy was made of many of the plates, and in the eighteenth century this copy was acquired by Sir Joseph Banks and is now in the British Museum (Natural History). The drawings of plants are excellent but those of the birds are rather crude; they are of exceptional interest, however, since at least one folio of these bird drawings (see Plate 2) is missing from the original Viennese *Codex*.

When the Roman Empire fell, the contents of the great libraries, as well as the scholars associated with them, were dispersed. Most of the accumulated knowledge of the Greeks and Romans would have vanished had it not been for the rise of the Arabs who absorbed both the ancient lore of Persia and the classical heritage of Greece and Rome. Arabic became the language of diplomacy and learning throughout most of the civilized world; the Arabs created their own independent ways of thought and creative research in astronomy, mathematics, geography and linguistics. Their translations from the Greek changed and transmuted much ancient learning; it was therefore never completely lost. The translation of Aristotle's zoological books from Arabic into Latin provided the impetus for the Emperor Frederick's work on falconry (Plate 5) in the thirteenth century. The modern science of ornithology developed slowly and steadily from that time.

Frederick II, of Hohenstaufen (1194–1250), Holy Roman Emperor, King of Sicily and Jerusalem, was passionately interested in falconry. A man of high intelligence, able to speak six languages, a skilful soldier, politician and diplomat, he attracted some of the best minds of the day to his court at Palermo. He is said to have developed an interest in Aristotle through Michael Scot, a man some twenty years older, mathematician, astrologer and translator. Scot had studied at Oxford and Paris and is believed to have been in his turn a pupil of the great medieval scholar Grosseteste (1175–1253). He spent some time at the court at Toledo where he learnt Arabic and translated Aristotle's works from that language into Latin for the Emperor Frederick.

Frederick spent thirty years accumulating facts for his great work entitled *De Arte Venandi cum Avibus*. His knowledge of falconry was partly based on an Arabic manuscript by Moamym, and partly on a Persian study of the sparrowhawk translated from Latin into French by Daniel of Cremona. Frederick himself was an accurate observer and his book contains accounts of migration, anatomy, the mechanism of flight and other ornithological matters. His own manuscript was lost after his defeat at the battle of Parma, but his son rewrote the book from his father's original notes and illustrations, and it was from this version that the surviving manuscripts were prepared. Frederick is believed to have made his own drawings and there are nine hundred marginal illustrations in the Vatican copy of his manuscript.

Fabulous birds still had their devotees at this time, and they continued well into the era of the printed book. Slightly younger than the Emperor Frederick was Albertus Magnus (?1206–80), Bishop of Regensburg, teacher of Thomas Aquinas, but more important in this context as the man who above all was responsible for the introduction of Aristotelian thought in all its complexities into western Europe; he was incidentally a very good naturalist himself. A work entitled *The Boke of secretes of Albartus Magnus, of the virtues of herbes, stones and certaine beastes*, published in London in 1525, is most probably not by him. It contains observations such as: 'The Lapwynge or Black Plover is a bird sufficiently knowen . . . and if thou shalt have the heade of it in thy purse, thou canst not be deceived of any merchaunt. This hath ben proved this daye of our brethren.' It seems scarcely likely that this great thinker and scholar who would have no truck with the fable of the Barnacle Goose, would have set down this and other fabulous descriptions which are to be found in *The Boke of secretes*.

One of the most popular manuscripts of the thirteenth century was *De Proprietatibus Rerum*, written before 1260 by an Englishman Bartholomaeus Anglicus. It was originally translated into French by Jean Corbichon in 1372 by order of King Charles V, and also into Spanish, Dutch and English. It was a compilation in nineteen books of the knowledge of the day, and the successor to one compiled by Isidore of Seville in AD 623, in fact a kind of popular encyclopedia. It contains a section on flying animals which includes insects as well as birds. The phoenix and griffon still make their appearance, but there are authentic and original observations, including a delightful description of the stridulating mechanism of the cicada, which shows that the writer had some knowledge of the respiratory system of these insects. *De Proprietatibus Rerum* retained its popularity after the invention of printing, and no less than ten editions in Latin were published in the fifteenth century, as well as four in French, and one each in Dutch, Spanish and English.

Printing and the increase in the use of paper, which had been invented by the Chinese in the second century AD but took several centuries to spread to the West, made available all the current knowledge of birds and their habits. Hitherto, with a few notable exceptions such as the works of Frederick II and Bartholomaeus Anglicus, birds had been used largely as decorative symbols in medieval manuscripts and embroideries. Over and over again the crane was depicted, together with the woodpecker (associated with the myths of the thunder bird), the wren with its own share of myth, blue tits, swans, peacocks, and the hawk striking a mallard drake. We can see them all in the Fitzwilliam Bird Psalter in Cambridge, which is thought to be of the early fourteenth century, and in others of an earlier date. Another manuscript of a different type, in the Pepysian Library in Cambridge (Plate 15), contains eight folios of birds; the rest of the volume consists of drawings of man and other animals in a variety of poses. This manuscript has been discussed at length by R. W. Scheller in a work on medieval model books, and more recently by G. E. Hutchinson in an article in *Isis*. As we have seen in the case of the ancient Egyptians, the artists employed certain conventions for representing birds, particularly when they had to depict certain difficult poses. These conventions were passed from one workshop to another. There is, for instance, a model book in Paris containing birds drawn by Pisanello which shows that this was the case in northern Italy, and probably throughout Europe.

Some illuminated manuscripts of the fourteenth century served quite a different purpose, for instance, the Sloane manuscript (Plates 9 and 10) which is apparently a kind of herbal; it includes animals useful as a source of drugs: a cricket, a lizard, a crane, a hawk and mallard locked in mid-air, and many others. Little is known of the provenance of this Italian manuscript save that it was acquired by Sir Hans Sloane, whose library and collections formed the nucleus of the British Museum when it was established in the eighteenth century. It may be a survival from a long line of similar works, featuring the sources of avian drugs among others.

As a contrast, if we turn to Plates 7 and 8 showing details from the Sherborne Missal, written by John Whas, and illuminated by John Siferwas for the Bishop of Salisbury and the Abbot of Sherborne between 1396 and 1407, we shall find that it seems to have a new purpose. The decoration and lettering are magnificent but the birds are painted with an accuracy hitherto almost unknown. A great variety are shown and carefully labelled; they include the blackbird, linnet, heron, swan, starling, shrike, jay, cock and hen sparrow, cock and hen chaffinch, coal-tit, sheldrake, moorhen, lark, goldfinch, peacock and others. It seems clear that the artist's purpose was didactic as well as decorative, and this is emphasized by the casual treatment of bees, grasshoppers, butterflies and other insects in the same missal. Siferwas has included several portraits of himself and the scribe in Dominican habits, and it may be that the Dominicans had a traditional interest in natural history. Albertus Magnus was one of them.

After the invention of printing a certain number of manuscripts continued to be copied by professional scribes, and were often ornamented with elaborate marginal paintings. An artist working in the Netherlands illuminated a Book of Hours for Mary of Burgundy (1457–82) who died as a result of a hunting accident when she was only twenty-five years old. This volume, now in the Bodleian Library, contains some of the finest natural history illuminations of any age. There is a memorable Annunciation with a richly sombre border of peacock's feathers; on other pages there are flowers, shells, and insects including dragonflies, butterflies and moths in all sorts of poses. In the section illustrated with hunting scenes there are a number of birds but, while some are fairly accurate, others combine the features of one or more species; Siferwas is outstanding in comparison.

Although engraving on metal was practised in the fifteenth century, the earliest printed books relied on woodcuts for their illustrations and these fell far short of the accomplishment of the old illuminators; by the end of the sixteenth century the engravers' techniques had improved to a remarkable degree, and steel and copper engraving had become acceptable media for reproduction.

Amongst the early printed books is an edition of Bartholomaeus Anglicus printed in Haarlem by Jacopo Bellaert in 1485, more than two hundred years after it was written, and fifteen years later than a Basle edition that has no woodcuts. The plate that embellished the section on birds in Bellaert's edition is a spirited rendering of many familiar birds including the hoopoe, swallow, parrot, pheasant, peacock, green plover, crane, heron, magpie, eagle, shoveler and other ducks. There is also a standard representation of a phoenix and a griffon, two of the fabulous birds of antiquity.

In his *Dictionary of Birds* (1893–6), Alfred Newton tells us that to doubt the existence of the phoenix was for long regarded as evidence of depravity. In western mythology it was reputed to be the only one of its kind. Resplendent to look at, it lived in the Arabian desert for six hundred years, then burnt itself to death on an aromatic pyre ignited by the sun. From the ashes it rose to live another six hundred years. One of the first accounts of this creature came from Hesiod, about the eighth century BC, and another from Herodotus about 484–425 BC; a 'very learned scholar' in Oxford is reputed to have maintained a belief in it as late as 1840. Perhaps it had been made acceptable to him through the words of Job: 'Then I said I shall die in my nest and I shall multiply my days as the phoenix.'

The Chinese also had a mythical phoenix. About 2700 BC the emperor Huang Ti, said to have lived one hundred years, ordered a minister Ling Lun to establish the correct pitch for music. In high mountains to the west Ling Lun found suitable bamboos with nodes of uniform thickness from which he cut twelve pipes which he grouped in sixes according to the songs of the male and female phoenix in the mountain woods. From these were cast twelve bells so that splendid music might be made. One of the oldest Chinese musical instruments is the *cheng*, said to represent a phoenix with folded wings. The body of the bird is the sounding box, and the surrounding pipes are its voice.

The griffon, supposed to have the body of a lion, the wings of an eagle and a hooked beak, had a very different fate. The Greeks believed that it guarded the gold of the Scythians. In 1666 its name was transferred by some French scientists to a vulture they had dissected, so that ultimately it assumed a perfectly valid existence. The name is now applied to members of the genus *Gyps*.

Bellaert's illustration (Plate 11) seems to have been much admired. It was copied by Wynkyn de Worde, Caxton's foreman, for his 1495 edition of *De Proprietatibus Rerum*, and the following year for his edition of Juliana Barnes's *Boke of St Albans*, a compilation on hunting and hawking that was first printed, unillustrated, in St Albans in 1486. The plates in both these books are identical in every respect; they are mirror images of Bellaert's original design, but have been simplified and are cruder and less attractive.

A block of somewhat similar character (Plate 13) forms the frontispiece to the 1526 edition of Chaucer's *Assemble of Foules*, produced by Rycharde Pynson, the King's printer.

Some of the most delightful illustrations of birds appeared about this time in the early editions of *Aesop's Fables*, many of which had elaborate borders in imitation of the illuminated manuscripts that were still being produced in most European countries.

Minor authors in the sixteenth century include Olaus Magnus (1490–1558), Archbishop of Sweden, who wrote an account of the Scandinavian people, *Historia de Gentibus Septentrionalibus*, which was published in Rome in 1555. He supported the existence of the mythological kraken but his work contains some interesting material and some very vigorous small woodcuts in which he groups various birds according to their habits. Among the best known is one of fishermen (Plate 37) drawing up their nets which contain (supposedly) hibernating swallows as well as a draught of fishes. Well into the nineteenth century many intelligent men supported the idea that these birds hibernated under water, partly because they tend to become torpid in very cold weather, and partly because they congregate over water on account of the abundance there of flies with aquatic larvae.

By the early sixteenth century curious birds from far lands were becoming known to Europeans, and there was a great and growing interest in them. Lourenço Diaz discovered the Guinea hornbill in 1477; Oviedo, who sailed with Columbus, wrote an account of the natural history of the West Indies, the earliest edition of which seems to be one of 1526. Oviedo briefly described boobies, the storm petrels that accompanied the ships for much of the Atlantic crossing, and, in the Caribbean area, the impressive frigate-birds, the Tropic Birds later to be so appropriately named *Phaethon aethereus*, the pelicans, and other more familiar birds. He also commented on the vast numbers of large birds to be seen on migration during March.

Pigafetta, who sailed with Magellan on the first circumnavigation 1518–21, observed giant colonies of penguins in Patagonia and brought the first skins of birds of paradise (minus their legs) from the Moluccas to Europe.

From 1571 to 1577 Dr Francisco Hernández assembled notes and drawings on all aspects of natural history and native life in Mexico for Philip II of Spain. These were bound into fifteen large illustrated volumes but all were lost in a fire in the Escorial in 1671. Some of the illustrations were reproduced in *Thesauri rerum Medicarum Novae Hispaniae* (ed. Johann Faber) in 1628. The example of the Spaniards stimulated Richard Hakluyt, the elder, to insist that on a North American expedition 'a skilful painter is also to be carried with you, which the Spaniards commonly used in all their discoveries to bring the descriptions of all beasts, birds, fishes, trees, townes etc'. A Portuguese pilot wrote of Drake (on his voyage around the world 1577–80) that: 'He kept a book in which he entered his navigation and in which he delineated birds, trees and sea lions. He is adept in painting and has with him a boy, a relative of his, who is a great painter. When they both shut themselves up in his cabin they were always painting.'

These various stimuli provided an atmosphere in which ornithology could develop as a serious science and there were three outstanding men in the sixteenth century who took advantage of the general interest and by their work put the science on a new footing. They were Gesner, a Swiss, Belon, a Frenchman, and Aldrovandi, a Bolognese.

The greatest of this trio was Conrad Gesner (1515–65) whose *Historia Animalium* covers the whole field of sixteenth-century zoology. He corresponded with zoologists including William Turner (1508–68) the first writer on British birds. He published names of animals, with their ancient and modern equivalents, and included biological as well as bibliographical information. Gesner was the first to emphasize the value of illustrations as an aid to the study of zoology, and he himself provided many of the figures in his book. His work was that of a pioneer in many ways, and it remained authoritative until the time of Ray and Willughby a hundred years later.

Gesner studied the classics, science and medicine at Basle, Paris and Montpellier. He loved the mountains and was one of the early alpinists with many ascents to his credit. He was appointed to a Chair at Zurich where in 1564 he overworked during an epidemic of plague; the following year there was another outbreak and as he had not recovered his strength he died as a result. He was the founder of bibliography as well as one of the most important figures in the development of zoology.

His almost exact contemporary, Pierre Belon (1517–64), was born at Le Mans. He too had wide interests, and was a close friend of the poet Ronsard. Among his writings is a work of aquatic animals; much of his information was derived from his observations at the fish markets of the Mediterranean towns which he toured extensively, visiting North Africa as well as Greece and Turkey. His classification of fishes was of fundamental value and we probably owe to him the introduction of the Lebanese Cedar to Europe. His *Histoire de la nature des Oyseaux*, published in Paris in 1555, is one of the foundation stones of comparative anatomy. Aristotle had compared the uterus in a number of species; Belon published parallel figures of the skeletons of a man and a bird, relating the homologous bones to each other. (Nearly one hundred and fifty years later Edward Tyson, in his work *Orang-Outang, or the Anatomy of a Pigmie compared with that of a Monkey, an Ape, and a Man*, London 1699, made another comparative study in which he introduced the concept that man was akin to certain lower animals, a theory which through Darwin's work was so radically to change human thought.) Belon also classified birds according to their habits and structure. His output of published work was remarkable considering that his life was fairly short; he was killed by robbers in the Bois de Boulogne under mysterious circumstances.

Ulisse Aldrovandi (1522–1605) studied philosophy and medicine in Padua and Rome, then returned to his birthplace to be Professor, first of Botany and then of Natural History. He amassed vast collections; his great work *Historiam Naturalem in Gymnasio Bononiensi profitensis Ornithologiae . . .* was completed by pupils and friends from his manuscripts after his death. The first three volumes, on birds, were published under his own supervision in 1599, and a fourth, on insects, appeared in 1602. Less critical than Gesner, his publications were rather more complete and he profited from Gesner's example in that he spared no trouble to procure the best possible illustrations for his books; the story of those of the various forms of ruff in breeding plumage is an example of this (Plates 33 and 34).

Ornithology continued to develop in the seventeenth century. In 1622 G. P. Olina published a book on Italian birds. His *Uccelliera overo discorso della natura . . .* was lavishly provided with woodcuts showing not only single birds, sometimes with their food, but also methods of trapping and hunting. In one scene a mounted huntsman is holding an owl, used as a lure since it is mobbed by other species when it appears in daylight; other men are ready to release their falcons to seize the attackers. Olina also shows a man hidden in a cow's skin, with the head of the animal still attached, approaching flocks of birds that have been attracted by ground-bait; this plate does not appear in all editions of his work. He also illustrated ways of encouraging caged nightingales to sing and, on the next page, the preparation of these same birds for pies. Perhaps this was another case of sympathetic magic: and Italian singers may have believed their voices might be strengthened by such delicacies. It is in any case an example of the extraordinary ambivalence shown by many nations to birds which are greatly loved as pets but almost as greatly appreciated as targets for the skilled marksman or victims for the trapper.

The major advance in scientific ornithology in the seventeenth century was due to the fundamental ideas on classification put forward by Ray and Willughby. John Ray (1628–1705) was a very good naturalist, both practical and theoretical. He was primarily a botanist, while his friend and pupil, Francis Willughby (1635–72) was an ornithologist and ichthyologist. They worked together very closely and when Willughby died at the age of thirty-seven, Ray edited and added to his work on birds, and then published it. Together they worked out a scheme of classification far in advance of anything put forward by Belon and his contemporaries. Later Ray published a classification of plants, and of insects and vertebrates. He wrote prolifically and on a wide range of non-biological subjects.

The two friends travelled widely on the continent and amongst the naturalists they met was a certain L. Baldner of Strasburg. Since he lived at the junction of three rivers Baldner had made a special study of the water-birds and fishes of the neighbourhood, and had employed a local artist to paint them. The English travellers, greatly impressed by his work, bought a volume of paintings and manuscripts from him, and Ray had the latter translated. Baldner had copies made which remained in Germany, but these do not compare in quality or treatment with the originals now in the British Museum (Plates 65, 66).

In the seventeenth century there was no technique of colour printing, and illustrations continued to be coloured by hand until the end of the eighteenth century.

Well before this, however, some gifted colourists began to work on natural history subjects. One of the most able of these painters was Maria Sybille Merian (1647–1717) who in her fifties visited Surinam to paint the insects and smaller vertebrates of that country in their natural surroundings. Her magnificent plates of flowers and insects are well known, but her bird paintings, now in the British Museum, appear to have been overlooked. She used the same technique for painting birds as for her other work but appears to have been sometimes carried away, and then added embellishments, such as the caruncles on the primaries of the Muscovy Duck (Plate 1), which are entirely imaginary.

It was becoming commercially viable to produce large illustrated bird books by this time. There were considerable scientific advances throughout the eighteenth century which also provided a stimulus for ornithological publications. Classification which had been established on a sound basis by Ray and Willughby was reorganized on a grand scale by Linnaeus (1707–78) who developed his methods by attention to ways of classifying books. Linnaeus was enormously industrious and his work covered the whole kingdom of biology, though he was primarily a botanist. With such a vast range to cover he was naturally much better in dealing with some groups than with others. Thomas Pennant, the outstanding British zoologist of the eighteenth century, wrote to Joseph Banks when he was preparing to visit Linnaeus in Sweden: 'I sincerely wish your tour may answer but not being greatly smitten with the charms of Linnaeus, must be doubtful until I hear from you. As to ornithology he is too superficial to be thought of, in madrepology still more deficient.' Nevertheless, Linnaeus established a zoological foundation on which others could work, and he inspired many able pupils, who travelled widely and made outstanding contributions to biological science.

Against this essential background of classification, books began to appear on the ornithology of regions that had hitherto been treated in a fragmentary fashion. Catesby, an Englishman by birth, published his *Natural History of Carolina* (1731–43), the first comprehensive account of the fauna and flora of North America, with descriptions of more than a hundred species of birds. As noted elsewhere in this volume, he used seven of the illustrations of birds drawn by John White (see Plate 21) of the Roanoke expedition, only one of which bears White's name; Linnaeus used four of these drawings to illustrate types of American birds but he attributed them to Catesby.

Eleazar Albin wrote a more general work, *A Natural History of Birds* (1731–38), the first illustrated book on British birds, with some foreign species. A much more comprehensive undertaking was George Edwards's *A Natural History of Uncommon Birds* (1743–51), which was printed in parallel columns of French and English and immediately went into a second edition. Both these books were well illustrated; Edwards revised an edition of Catesby's book as well as writing his own. He used to borrow exotic birds from many sources and his notes on the pets kept by members of the nobility, by doctors and in London taverns are very amusing and interesting. There was, for instance, a Great Horned Owl from Hudson's Bay, which was kept as a pet at the Mourning Bush Tavern in Aldersgate.

The most profound work on birds in the eighteenth century was perhaps that of Buffon, whose approach to biology was more philosophical than that of his predecessors. He recognized the universal character of living matter, and wrote a magnificent *Histoire Naturelle des Oiseaux*, consisting of ten volumes that appeared from 1771 to 1786 and were lavishly illustrated in colour.

While Buffon's work was being produced, another manuscript, based on the circumnavigations of Captain Cook, was in preparation. It was planned to contain a comprehensive survey of the oceanic birds of the world, and the land birds of parts of South America, the Pacific islands, Australasia, Java, the Cape of Good Hope and Hawaii. The scientific work was done jointly by two men, Joseph Banks, and Daniel Solander who was a favourite pupil of Linnaeus; Banks had also a team of trained artists. Hundreds of copperplates of the plants they had collected on the voyage of the *Endeavour* were made and years were spent drafting and arranging the descriptions of both plants and animals but, when most of the work was done, Solander died suddenly. Banks, overcome by grief in the first place, and then preoccupied by many other responsibilities (he was President of the Royal Society for over forty years), never published the work although he made all his collections and manuscript material available to other scientists. He had, however, set an example of sending scientists with trained artists and reasonable equipment on voyages of exploration. So the precedent set so long before by the Spaniards and by Drake was at last implemented and led to the establishment of famous research ships such as the *Challenger* in the following century.

Some of the birds collected by Banks and Solander were published by their English friends, such as John Latham who wrote *A General Synopsis of Birds* (1781–1802), and Thomas Pennant whose *Arctic Zoology* was one of the first books on zoogeography to be published; it included descriptions and uncoloured engravings of a large number of birds. Pennant's *British Zoology* was a folio volume with large and vigorous paintings by Peter Paillou who excelled in depicting birds of prey and game-birds (Plates 89 and 90).

In 1798 lithography was invented, a development which was to have far-reaching importance for the production of natural history books of all kinds, and eventually led to the worst excesses of chromo-lithography. At the same time wood-engraving gained fresh vitality, firstly from the innovations of Thomas Bewick (1753–1828), one of the most expert of all engravers, whose work has never been surpassed for strength, delicacy and charm, and secondly from the mastery of the medium by the great Japanese artist Hokusai Katsushika (1760–1849) who, on his death-bed at the age of eighty-nine, said, 'If Heaven had lent me but five years more I should have become a great painter.'

The increase in knowledge of the birds of countries new to European eyes, and the simplification of the processes of colour printing led to the production of lavishly illustrated bird books on a very large scale indeed throughout the nineteenth century. There were books on the birds of South America, Africa, Asia, Australia and New Guinea; monographs on humming-birds running into many volumes; others on pheasants and birds of paradise. Superb artists painted them, far too many to list here, though perhaps we should mention Edward Lear, whose parrots are unforgettable and whose birds, even in the books of nonsense, are wonderfully accurate in character, and also Gould, for whom Lear did many drawings. Gould was fortunate in marrying a wife who became an even better artist than he was himself; he named a charming little Australian finch after her. Keulemans worked for many of the noted collectors of this time, and in India lonely English soldiers and civil servants, such as Hodgson, Tickell and Sharpe, occupied their leisure with the study of ornithology, sometimes employing Indian artists, who had a long heritage of painting, to work for them. In North America Wilson and Audubon diligently recorded a great number of birds; in South America Descourtilz made spectacular use of the food plants or prey of his birds to illustrate one of the most beautiful of all bird books.

It was a superb climax to the preceding centuries but man's intrusion into the remote habitats occupied by so many of the most beautiful species was doomed to be destructive. In the eighteenth century Great Auks were so numerous on the Newfoundland Banks that they were figured as indicators of that area in the fourth book of *The English Pilot* (1767). Only a few years later, Banks's friend, Major George Cartwright, commented on the destruction by fishermen of the colonies breeding on Funk Island: 'If a stop is not soon put to that practice, the whole breed will be diminished to almost nothing, particularly the penguins [i.e. Great Auks]: for this is now the only island they have left to breed upon: all the others lying so near the coast of Newfoundland, they are continually robbed. The birds which the people bring from thence, they salt and eat, in lieu of salted pork.' In less than one hundred years the birds had become entirely extinct.

Alfred Russell Wallace, the first to watch birds of paradise and make extensive notes on their behaviour, wrote on similar lines:

It seems sad that on the one hand these exquisite creatures should live out their lives and exhibit their charms only in these wild inhospitable regions, doomed for ages yet to come to hopeless barbarism; while on the other hand, should civilised man ever reach these distant lands, and bring moral, intellectual and physical light into the recesses of these virgin forests, we may be sure that he will so disturb the nicely-balanced relations of organic and inorganic nature as to cause the disappearance, and finally the extinction of these very beings whose wonderful structure and beauty he alone is fitted to appreciate and enjoy! This consideration must surely tell us that all living things were not made for man.

The era of the great illustrated bird books is over, and the millions of bird skins in the national museums should now be more than adequate for all the remaining systematic work that is necessary to determine relationships of the more obscure groups. The living birds left to us deserve our protection; they still present us with extremely difficult problems concerned with the various aspects of migration, communication between the members of vast flocks, and other facets of behaviour. If the collection of plates and records in this book stimulates interest in the care and protection of these remarkable animals it will have served one of its chief purposes; in addition it is to be hoped that this selection of plates will give readers at least some of the pleasure that the author has felt in looking through many hundreds of the bird books of past centuries.

PLATES
&NOTES

1

Muscovy Duck *(Cairina moschata)*

Plate 78 from a volume of watercolour paintings by Maria Sybille
Merian, undated, British Museum

Maria Sybille Merian (1647–1717) was one of the finest natural history
painters of the second part of the seventeenth century. She was born
in Germany; her father was the well-known Swiss engraver Matthäus
Merian, and her mother the daughter of another accomplished engraver,
a Dutchman, J. T. de Bry. When Matthäus died his widow married a
Dutch flower painter Jacob Marrell, one of whose pupils, Johann Graff,
married Maria when she was seventeen years old. With such a background
she had every opportunity to develop her great natural talents. Her
first book, a three-volume work on European insects, began to appear
in 1679; the illustrations were engraved and coloured by herself, with
assistance, it is said, from her younger daughter Dorothea. In 1685 she
joined the followers of a French pietist and left her husband. The
Labadist community made its headquarters in Friesland, and it was there
that she saw a collection of insects from Surinam which inspired her to
visit that country. So in 1698 she set out, with Dorothea, for South
America where she spent nearly two years before poor health compelled
her to return to Europe. Her book *Metamorphosis Insectorum
Surinamensium* (1705) is a marvellously rich publication, and rightly
famous, but the fact that she also painted birds both in Surinam and
Europe is little known. There are thirteen paintings of birds in the
volume in the British Museum from which this painting of the Muscovy
Duck is taken. It is slightly surrealist in treatment since there are far too
many caruncles; only the male mallard, and ordinary domestic ducks
which derive from mallards, possess the curl over the tail with which she
has embellished this bird. It has not been possible to identify the snake;
she was clearly fascinated by these reptiles and several of her bird
paintings include one or more of them in highly decorative positions.

Watercolour with some kind of varnish on vellum, 15 × 12·9 in.
(381 × 329 mm.)

2, 3
Various birds

Folios 416 and 412 from a manuscript copy (*c.* 1458–77) of the *Dioscorides Codex*, British Museum (Natural History)

These two plates are from the zoological section of a copy of the Juliana Anicia version (AD 512) of the *Dioscorides Codex*, now in Vienna. There are five folios of snakes and other reptiles, some arachnids and insects, and six of birds many of which have their Greek names written in. The watermark on the paper is a pair of scissors which enables it to be dated with some precision. The endpapers are splendidly designed in gold and maroon on white and the whole is bound in vellum. The paintings of plants which constitute the major part of the volume are very handsome, and richly coloured. The zoological section is much less finely executed, and gives the impression of being a copy, several times removed, from a manuscript of considerable antiquity. The volume was acquired by Sir Joseph Banks in 1782 from the sale of the library of Jacobi Soranzo in Padua.

Discorides, an army doctor in the reign of Nero, compiled a great herbal, based on the *Materia Medica* of the day, and more especially on a much earlier illustrated work by Krateuas, body-physician to Mithridates VI Eupator (120–63 BC) who is said to have had an unrivalled knowledge of poisons and their antidotes. Pliny, writing of the herbals with which he was familiar, stated: 'Euax, a king of the Arabians, wrote a book as touching the virtues and operations of Simples which he sent into the Emperor Nero. Crateuas likewise, Dionysius also, and Metrodorus, wrote of the same Argument after a most pleasant and plausible manner . . . they painted every herb in their colours.'

The Dionysius to whom Pliny refers may have been a Greek of that name who was associated with Ptolemy II, the second Greek king of Egypt (309/8–246 BC), who had the nickname Philadelphus–brother-loving. This nickname has erroneously led to Dionysius being labelled as coming from Philadelphia in Amman. Various authorities ascribe the bird paintings in the *Dioscorides Codex* to that Dionysius. He is in any case a vague and shadowy figure.

The paintings are all in shades of buff, umber and grey; the fish-eating gull has a pink bill and feet. The birds of prey on Plate 3 (folio 412) are not represented in the Viennese manuscript. There is no doubt about the identity of the two birds at the bottom of Plate 2; the pelican on the left is unmistakable, so is the kingfisher, *Alcyon*, on the right. The bird on the top right of the page is called *Trochilos*, now used for humming-birds owing to some confusion in the mind of Linnaeus, but anciently it was applied to the smaller plovers, and particularly to the Crocodile Bird, *Pluvianus aegyptius*. The other birds cannot be identified with any certainty. The Viennese manuscript contains notes on trapping birds and some observations on their habits; these are missing from the British Museum copy.

Watercolours, each 10 × 7·75 in. (254 × 202 mm.)

4
Various birds

Plate [1] from *Das Buch der Natur*, by Konrad (Conrad) von Megenburg, Augsburg, 1481 (first edition 1475)

Konrad (*c.* 1309–74) studied in Erfurt, then went to Paris where he became a magister, and studied philosophy and theology. After eight years in Paris he moved to Vienna, and finally to Regensburg where he spent most of his life. Konrad was the first great scientist to write in the German tongue and he was particularly interested in the education of women and the common man. His influence was very considerable through his translation of Thomas of Cantimpré's encyclopedia, *De natura rerum*, a popular work. Thomas of Cantimpré was a Flemish Dominican who lived from about 1200 to between 1270 and 1280 and was thus a contemporary of Bartholomaeus Anglicus, whose encyclopedia was even more successful (see pp. 16, 17 and Plates 11 and 12).

Das Buch der Natur contains a long section on animals, including many chapters on birds entitled *Von der Vogeln in einer Gemeyn* for which the woodcut opposite is the frontispiece. Many manuscript copies of this work were made before the introduction of printing. The first edition of 1475 is believed to be the earliest work to contain printed illustrations of animals.

Woodcut, 7 × 5 in. (178 × 127 mm.)

5
Various birds

Marginal illustration from folio 8r of *De Arte Venandi cum Avibus*, by Frederick II of Hohenstaufen, Holy Roman Emperor, King of Sicily and Jerusalem

The Emperor Frederick spent thirty years amassing material for his book which contains a great variety of general ornithological material as well as technical information on falconry. There are nine hundred marginal illustrations in the Vatican manuscript, which are thought to be copies of his work. His own manuscript was lost in battle and surviving copies are based on one now in the Vatican Museum (Pal. Lat. 1071) prepared by his son from the original notes; this illustration is taken from a modern facsimile.

Through the translations of Michael Scot (p. 16), Frederick became familiar with the zoological works of Aristotle which he tested and criticized. He was an outstanding polymath, a scientist, philosopher, linguist and administrator; many scholars, both Christian and Muslim, were attracted to his court. His book is remarkable for providing the first records of the air spaces in the bones of birds, the structure of the lungs, other anatomical features and the mechanics of flight; he also noted some of the facts of migration.

The Greylag Goose, swan and pelican in the upper row illustrate the statement made in the accompanying text that swimming water-birds often sleep standing on one leg in the water and that almost all, like the swan, lay their heads between the shoulder blades. The heron on the right represents the waders that do not swim but also pass the night standing in the water.

Watercolour on vellum, 3·75 × 5·25 in. (95 × 134 mm.)

6

Finch-billed Bulbul *(Spizixos semitorques)*

Detail from a Chinese painted scroll, undated, Department of Oriental
Antiquities, British Museum

This painting, and another version which is part of the National Palace
Collection in Taipei, Taiwan, are possibly by the famous painter-
emperor Hui-tsung (1082–1135), but it is uncertain whether it is
actually from his own hand or from that of one of the many gifted
artists who were attracted to his court, and learnt his technique. He
appears to have been a weak but amiable man, prodigal in his expenditure
of public money which he used partly to build up huge collections of
rocks and other natural formations. He had a large aviary and was
particularly interested in painting birds with as much naturalistic detail
as possible, but he had a great regard for composition and an astonishing
feeling for colour. Much early Sung painting reflects his influence. He
came to the throne in 1101 and reigned until 1125 when China was
invaded by the Chin Tartars who captured his capital, and carried him
and 3000 members of his court to Mongolia where he died in 1135.

The invaders destroyed or dispersed much of his collections, but a
catalogue survived of the paintings he had accumulated and this contained
6396 titles, the work of over two hundred artists.

Bulbuls are widely distributed in many parts of Africa, southern and
eastern Asia, and in Malaysia. They are usually gregarious, and some are
good songsters.

Watercolour on silk, 11 × 114 in. (280 × 2810 mm.)

7, 8

Teal *(Anas crecca)*
Wren *(Troglodytes troglodytes)*
Details from folios 27 and 371 of the Sherborne Missal, illuminated
by John Siferwas 1396–1407

This missal, originally prepared for the Benedictine Abbey of St Mary,
Sherborne, Dorset, and now in the library of the Duke of Northumberland
at Alnwick, may be regarded as the first sustained attempt in England
to draw and identify birds in number, with the object of making the
knowledge available for teaching purposes. Previously birds had been
drawn, sometimes in considerable detail, but primarily for purposes of
the decoration (see Plate 15 and p. 17) of embroideries and manuscripts
for which the English school was famous.

   Siferwas was a Dominican friar; there are several portraits of him in
this manuscript which is one of the most splendid in the whole history
of English illumination. A larger self-portrait may be seen in the Lovel
Lectionary, Harley MS 7026, in the British Museum, but there are few
birds in that document.

Watercolour on vellum; the details reproduced here are the original
size. The folios themselves are 21 × 15 in. (533 × 381 mm.)

9, 10
OVERLEAF

Crane *(Grus communis)*
Hawk and Mallard (Indet., *Anas platyrhyncha)*
Folios 42 and IIV from *Simplicia medicamonta* [sic] . . ., Sloane MS 4016,
British Museum

This ancient *Materia Medica* is a north Italian manuscript; some folios
showing men and girls can be dated from the costumes and belong to the
1370s; others appear to be at least half a century later. The crane was a
symbol of longevity and a favourite food at banquets. The hawk and
mallard seem perhaps to have strayed into this volume since this pose is
typically one found in illuminated manuscripts and embroideries.

Watercolour, each folio 14 × 10·25 in. (356 × 260 mm.)

11, 12
OVERLEAF

Various birds

Upper plate from *Boeck van den Proprieteyten der Dingen*, by Bartholomaeus
Anglicus, before 1260, published by Jacop Bellaert, Haarlem, 1485
Lower plate from *De Proprietatibus Rerum*, by Bartholomaeus Anglicus,
as above, published by Wynkyn de Worde, Westminster, 1495

Bartholomaeus was born an Englishman but later he studied and taught
in Paris. His book on the properties of matter was one of the most
widely read encyclopedias of the Middle Ages. Written before 1260, it
was translated into French in 1372, and into English by John of Trevisa
in 1398. It was this translation that Wynkyn de Worde, Caxton's foreman,

.Griles. sine locuste.

.Grus.

Grissomilia q̃ multi . baracheche appelãt aut mõla te.

Guara . i . maxi . figãtur . ⁊ salaman dras.

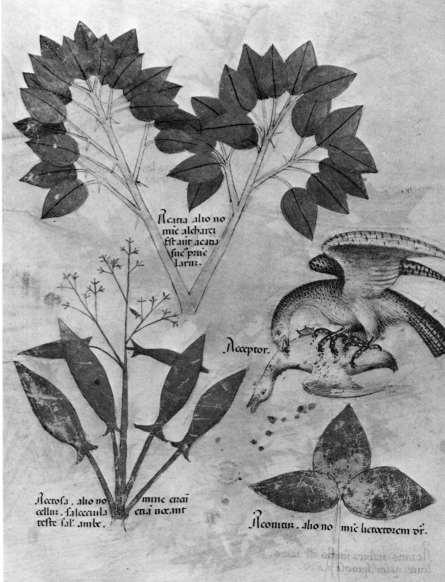

Acatia alio no mic alcharci est aut acatia suc̃ puc̃ laruz.

Acceptor.

Acetosa . alio no mine crai celluz . salecciula ena uocant teste sal. ambe.

Acomar . alio no mic hctcetorem di.

The lyfe fo fhort/ þ craft fo long to lerne
Thaffay fo harde/ fo fharpe the côqueryng
The flydder ioye/ þ alway flydde fo yerne
All this meane J by loue/that my felyng
Aftonyeth fo/ with a dredefull worzkyng

Of vfage/ what for luft/ what for lore
On bokes rede J ofte/as J you tolde
But why that J fpoke all this nat yore
J gone: it happed me for to beholde
Upon a boke / was writte with letters olde

cho camino al môte: donde hauia comido a fus côpañeros: τ como vieffe el can
cro de lexos los hueffos: penfando enfi el engaño y cautela del aue: delibero de

printed in 1495. The plate that faces the introduction to the section on birds is clearly based on the much more elaborate illustration used by Bellaert which has some delightful touches, such as the bittern among the reeds, and the various waders and ducks feeding and flapping their wings. Even Bellaert's fabulous birds have a convincing liveliness about their attitudes.

Wynkyn de Worde also used his plate in 1496 as a frontispiece to an edition of the *Boke of St Albans* by Dame Juliana Barnes, first printed at St Albans in 1486. This was a book of hawking and hunting which went into many editions.

Woodcuts, 7·85 × 5·3 in. (200 × 137 mm.) and 5·65 × 5·1 in. (145 × 130 mm.)

13

Various birds

Frontispiece to *The Assemble of Foules*, from *The Boke of Fame* etc., by Geffray Chaucer, part 2, London, 1526

The plate forming the frontispiece to the *Assemble of Foules*, in Rycharde Pynson's edition of this set of Chaucer's shorter poems, bears some resemblance to those printed by Bellaert and Wynkyn de Worde in their editions of Bartholomaeus Anglicus (Plates 11 and 12) but the birds are fewer in number and more crudely drawn.

Pynson's version of the famous opening lines of this poem begins thus:
The lyfe so short, ye craft so long to lerne
Thassay so harde so sharpe the conquering . . . .

Woodcut, 5·9 × 5·75 in. (150 × 147 mm.)

14

Eagle and lobster

Folio XVIIIv from *Exemplario contra los engaños : y peligros del mũdo* [a translation of a Latin version of the fables of Bidpai, the *Panchatantra*], by Joannes de Capua, Saragossa, 1531

This Spanish version of one of the fables of Bidpai, a Sanskrit collection of the third century, is based on a tale of a heron who, growing old and feeble, told the fishes and a crab in his pond that it was about to be drained, whereupon they asked him to carry them to another nearby. I have taken the liberty of modifying the translation (1925) by A. W. Ryder from the Sanskrit, so that his heron appears as the osprey (which never carries its prey in its bill) and the crab as the lobster: a lobster who had asked to be taken to safety with his friends the fishes, noticed that the osprey avoided water and was approaching a sun-scorched rock made horrible by heaps of fish skeletons.
Man is bidden to chastise even elders who devise
Devious courses, arrogant, of their duty ignorant.
Courageously he took heart.
Fear fearful things, while yet no fearful thing appears :
When danger must be met, strike and forget your fears.
'Before he drops me there', said the lobster to himself, 'I shall catch his neck with my claws.' He did so and cut off the osprey's head.

Woodcut, 4·35 × 5·7 in. (110 × 145 mm.)

15
Various birds

Plate 11b from the *Monk's Drawing Book*, undated, Magdalene College,
Cambridge

This fourteenth-century manuscript is one of the most interesting
medieval model books and the only surviving English example. A long
and detailed account of it was published in 1925 by M. R. James for
the Walpole Society, and more recently it was discussed by R. W.
Scheller in *A Survey of Medieval Model Books* (1963).

The whole collection consists of pages of drawings of human figures,
draperies, and various animals, the most remarkable of which are eight
pages of carefully drawn birds amongst which are scattered a few
irrelevant subjects such as the cat, the bat and the mermaid in the plate
reproduced here. It seems to have been used as a source book from
which designs for embroidery, and illuminated manuscripts could be
taken. Thus it has been shown that the bat can be traced to the Luttrell
Psalter and to a twelfth-century bestiary from Aberdeen. The gull occurs
in the thirteenth-century Tenison Psalter, and the hawk and duck locked
in mid-air may be seen in various other manuscripts including an Italian
herbal (see Plate 10).

Professor Alfred Newton wrote an account of the birds portrayed in
this model book, but unfortunately his paper seems to have been lost.
Tentative identifications were made many years afterwards by the late
N. B. Kinnear and A. H. Evans, who considered that the following birds
were represented in the plate printed here: skylark, yellow bunting,
cuckoo, and a second cuckoo or perhaps a nightjar, crane, spoonbill,
Greenland falcon, nightingale, lark and green woodpecker.

Watercolour on vellum, 9·8 × 7·4 in. (250 × 187 mm.)

APOLOGVS.

APOLOGVS.

16, 17, 18
Various birds

Plates of fables 2, 8 and 47 in *Libistici Fabulatores Esopi Vita Feliciter Incipit*, by Francesco del Tuppo, Naples, 1485

During the early decades of printing many woodcuts of animals appeared as illustrations to the fables of Aesop and Bidpai (Plate 14); some of these were brilliantly executed, as for instance these examples from Naples, although their chief purpose was to point a moral rather than depict some particular species. The text accompanying these plates is in Latin and Italian. The fables of the wolf and the crane, the cock and jewel are well known, but that of the sparrowhawk and nightingale is less familiar and part of Caxton's 1484 translation from a French edition is therefore given here:

He that oppresseth the Innocents shall have an evyl ende.
Esope refereth to us suche a fable of a sperehawk whiche dyd
put hym within the nest of a nyghtyngale where he fonde the
lytyl and yonge byrdes. The nyghtyngale came and perceyved hym,
wherfore she praid the sperehawke sayeng I requyre and praye the as
moche as I may that tholle have pyte on my smal byrdes And the
sperehawke answered and sayd yf tholle wylt that I graunte they
request tholle must synge swetely after my Wylle and gree And
thenne the nyghtyngale began to synge swetely not with the herte
but with the throte onely for he was too fylled of sorowe that
otherwyse he might not doo. The sperehawke sayd thenne to the
nyghtyngale This songe playseth me not And toke one of the
yonge byrdes and devoured hit. And as the sayd sperehawke would
have devoured and eten [the others] came there a hunter whiche
dyd caste a grete nette upon the sperehawke And whanne he wold
have fleen awey he might not for he was taken And therfore
he that doth harme and letteth the Innocents is worthy to
dye of evylle dethe.

More than three centuries later Bewick published his own illustrated versions of Aesop. His lines on the other two fables sum them up neatly:

> To fools, the treasures dug from wisdom's mine
> Are Jewels thrown to Cocks, and Pearls to Swine.

About the crane who was lucky to escape with his life after removing a fishbone from the wolf's throat:

> Who serves a villain might as wisely free
> The hardened murderer from the fatal tree.

Woodcuts, each approximately 6·3 × 4·9 in. (159 × 125 mm.)

19
Eagles
Drawings by Pisanello (Antonio Pisano), Print Room, British Museum

These two stylized representations of eagles, probably intended for
heraldic purposes, are by one of the most accomplished of the north
Italian artists of the later Middle Ages. Pisanello (*c.* 1395–1455) was
particularly gifted in portraying birds and made many studies of typical
poses. There is a sketchbook in the Bibliothèque Nationale showing
some of these; it may be classed with the model books discussed elsewhere
in this volume (pp. 15, 17).

Pen and ink and brown wash over black chalk on parchment, 8·6 × 6·1 in.
(222 × 155 mm.)

20

?Golden Eagle *(?Aquila chrysaëtos)*
Drawing by Il Parmigianino, Print Room, British Museum

This drawing by Parmigianino (1503–40) is believed to be a study for
the decoration of the vaulted ceiling of the north transept of Parma
Cathedral which he contracted to undertake when he was only nineteen
but never actually began. He was one of the most accomplished of the
Italian 'mannerist' artists of the sixteenth century, a prolific and brilliant
draughtsman.
    The eagle is the symbol for St John the Evangelist but this drawing is
less stylized than those by Pisanello above, and seems to be a portrait of a
living bird.

Red chalk on paper, 5·4 × 4·1 in. (137 × 105 mm.)

A Flaminco.

60

21

Flamingo *(Phoenicopterus ruber)*

Drawing by John White, *c.* 1585, Print Room, British Museum

This painting is by John White, the artist on the Roanoke expedition to Virginia, organized by Sir Walter Raleigh in 1585. White had a taste for exploration and is believed to have sailed in 1577 to Baffin Land with Frobisher on his second voyage in search of a north-west passage. His drawings of Virginia were largely used by de Bry in *America* (1590), who did not ascribe them to White but attached his own name to them as the engraver. Just over a century after White's death in about 1605, Sir Hans Sloane found a folio of his work in the possession of some descendants and had copies made, at least seven of which were used by Catesby (see Plates 45, 46) to illustrate his *Natural History of Carolina*; only one of these was acknowledged to White. Restitution was finally made in 1964, nearly four hundred years after the ill-fated Roanoke expedition, when all the known plates executed in Virginia were magnificently reproduced by the British Museum, under the editorship of P. H. Hulton and D. B. Quinn.

Flamingos are widely distributed in Europe, Asia, north Africa, and North and South America. Unfortunately the birds are nearly flightless when in moult and are then very vulnerable. They feed by filtering small organisms from the shallow waters where they congregate; their habitats tend to become restricted by wholesale reclamation projects. Wheeling flights of flamingos are spectacularly beautiful.

Watercolour on paper, 11·63 × 7·75 in. (296 × 197 mm.)

22

Skeletons of a crane *(Grus)*, starling *(Sturnus)*, woodpecker *(Picus)*, wryneck *(Jynx)*, cormorant *(Phalacrocorax carbo)* and a lizard *(Lacerta)*

Frontispiece to *Lectiones Gabrielis Fallopii . . .*, by Volcher Coeiter, Nuremberg, 1575

The ideas of Belon (p. 19 and Plate 48) on comparative anatomy obviously stimulated his contemporaries and this most interesting plate illustrates the second of two books by Coeiter (1534–76), the first scientist to publish a comparative work on anatomy covering the whole of the known vertebrate kingdom, excluding fishes. Coeiter was a Frisian by birth but studied in Italy and Montpellier; at the age of thirty he became professor of anatomy in Bologna, but he did not remain there long and returned to Germany. He studied the embryology of the human skeleton, and was the first scientist after Aristotle to publish an account of the development of the chick.

Engraving, 19 × 12 in. (370 × 485 mm.)

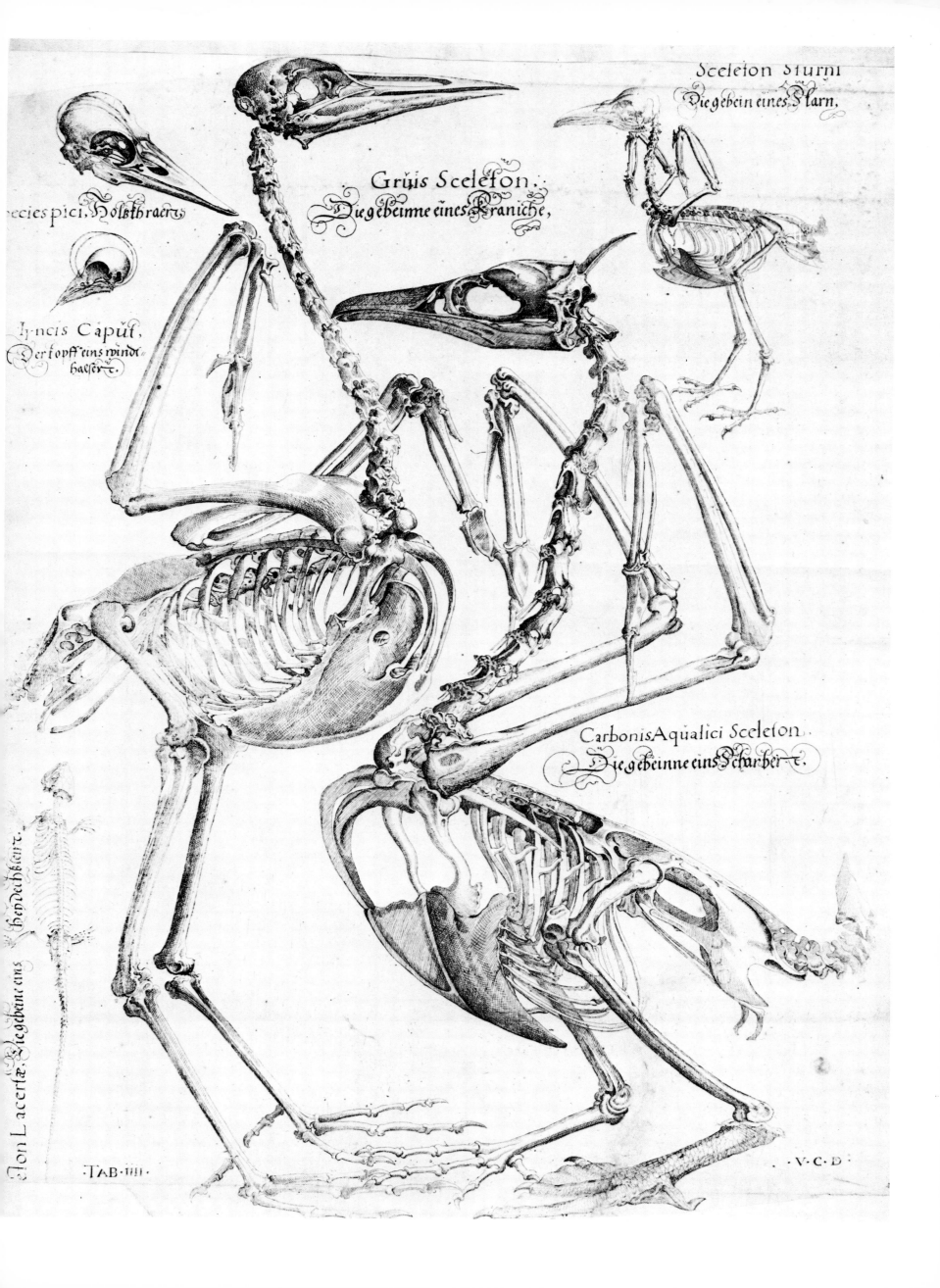

Sceleton Sturni
Die gebein eines Staarn.

Grüis Sceleton.
Die gebeinne eines Kraniche.

ecies pici, Holtzkraen.

Irncis Caput.
Der kopff eins windt
haese.

CarbonisAqualici Sceleton.
Die gebeinne eins Scharbe.

Von Lacertæ. Die gebeine eins Heydechseit.

TAB·IIII.

·V·C·D·

The Cock Hoopoe.

23

Hoopoe *(Upupa epops)*

Plate 42 from *Histoire Naturelle des Oiseaux . . .*, by Eleazar Albin, Vol. 2, The Hague, 1750

The hoopoe is a remarkably beautiful and conspicuous bird. It occurs from Europe to South Africa, India and across to Malaysia, usually in warm dry areas where there are open forest lands and an abundant supply of insects on which it mostly feeds.

Since hoopoes are relatively tame and have such striking plumage they have always tended to attract legends, from the time of Aristophanes who gave one a leading part in *The Birds*. In Arabia they were called the children of Solomon from a tradition that the Creator gave them crowns of gold for sheltering Solomon from the sun. They were so often killed for these crowns that they assembled and appealed to Solomon himself, who was so wise that he understood the language of all the animals. He prayed to the Creator to ameliorate their destiny whereupon the crown was changed to a crest of feathers of even greater beauty.

Albin was the first to write an illustrated account of British birds. The plate chosen here comes from the first French edition; the colouring varies from one copy to another, and is particularly rich in this set published in Holland. The first English edition was published 1731–8. Albin was a professional artist and with the help of his daughter Elizabeth drew and engraved all his own plates.

He also wrote a delightful history of song birds (1737) which contains many observations on their behaviour.

Engraving, 9·82 × 8·1 in. (250 × 205 mm.)

24, 25

Common Heron *(Ardea cinerea)*
Starling *(Sturnus vulgaris)*

Plates from pages 190 and 321 of *L'Histoire de la nature des Oyseaux
. . .*, by Pierre Belon, Paris, 1555

Pierre Belon (1517–64) is a key figure in the history of ornithology for
two reasons: he was one of the first to write a monograph on birds (he
also wrote one on fishes), and he was the first serious student of
comparative anatomy after Aristotle. Almost exactly contemporaneous
with Gesner (1516–65), he resembled him in the wide diversity of
interests that characterized his relatively short life (see also p. 19 and
Plate 48).

The woodcuts that illustrate his books were prepared by C. L.
Woeirot from drawings made by P. Gourdet. The two reproduced here
have a special interest since they show the birds with their food, a type
of illustration that was to be elaborated by ornithological artists in the
early part of the nineteenth century, some of whom, such as Audubon,
have been quite wrongly credited with initiating this kind of plate.

Woodcuts, 6·5 × 4·8 in. (165 × 122 mm.) and 5 × 4·5 in. (126 × 114 mm.)

26, 27

Pelican *(Pelecanus oncrotalus)*
Peacock *(Pavo cristatus)*

Plates from pages 605 and 631 of *Historia Animalium*, by Conrad
Gesner, Vol. III, Zurich, 1565

Gesner's importance in the development of zoology has been noted
elsewhere in this book (p. 19). He was the first to write a comprehensive
account of all the known animals, with reference to classical sources as
well as to current knowledge; his wide circle of scientific correspondents
in other European countries – he was born in Switzerland – gave him
great insight into a variety of subjects and many new zoological
observations were included in his *Historia Animalium* which was lavishly
illustrated. Jean Asper, Jean Thomas and Lucas Schroen were among the
artists who worked for him.

Woodcuts, 10 × 7 in. (254 × 178 mm.) and 6·9 × 7·5 in. (175 × 190 mm.)

nous tenons quelque petit chien pour côpagnië,que faisons coucher sur les pieds
de nostre lict pour plaisir : iceluy y auoit telles telles fois quelque animal priué es maisons
des païsans. Lon dit communement, que le Heron est viande Royale. Parquoy
la noblesse Françoyse fait grand cas de les manger, mais encor plus des Heron-
neaux : toutesfois les estrangers ne les ont en si grande recommandation . Il sont
Pellos & Herodios en Grec, Pella & Ardea en Latin, Heron en François.

O' πόλλοι οι ἐρωδιοὶ αρετρὴς φτοι χαλεπῶς ἐνιάζετη & ἡγρὴ κράζει τὴ...
μὴ ὀργῶσι, & ταῖς φωλεαῖς & ἰδίωμεσιν τὴ κορὰν ἐξ αύσσι πετομενὴ...
ἀλεκτουῶν. ὅταν χ αὐτοῖς & νύκτης. καὶ κρύφὴ τὴ γὴ καὶ αὐτοὶ κλίθλασι...
ὑπαγήσει τὴν φωσιν χρ μετ ἔχει ταὐτλα ἡ τῶν κεσαῖσι ἀειλ ὑγραῖς. Arist.lib.9.cap.1.& 18.

sans côparaison plus delicats que les Grues.Il apert par le vol qu'on dresse maintenant pour le Heron auec les oyseaux de proyë, que les anciens n'auoyent l'art
de fauconnerië si à main comme on l' à maintenant . Aristote à bien dit , au pre-
Combat mier chapitre , du neufiesme liure , que l'Aigle assaut le Heron , & qu'il meurt
du Heron en se deffendant.Le Heron se sentant assally,essaye à le gaigner en volant con-
auec l'Ai- tremont,& non pas au loing en suyant, comme quelques autres oyseaux de riuiè-
gle. re : & luy se sentant pressé,met son bec contremont par dessous l'ælle,sachant que
les oyseaux l'assomment de coups,dont aduient bien souuét qu'il en meurt plu-
sieurs

---

gendre bonnes humeurs,acomparants sa chair à celle de la Griue: aussi ont maintenant coustume de conceder aux malades d'en manger, l'estimants de facile
digestion.

De l'Estourneau.

CHAP. XXIX.

L'ESTOVRNEAV est tant cogneu d'vn chacû,qu'il n'est   *Estour-*
ia besoing d'en parler par le menu. Il à esté nommé des Grecs   *neau.*
Psaros, & en Latin *Sturnus.* Mais pource qu'il est taché, & à di-   *Psaros.*
uerses couleurs, & que la pierre Thebaïque, dont sont entail-   *Sturnus.*
lez les grands obelisques & grosses colosses des Egyptiens, est
quasi semblable en couleur à son plumage, les anciens nom-
meret icelle, pierre *Psaronium.* L'estourneau est vn peu plus petit que le Merle, aus
si est du nombre de ceux qu'on nourrist en cage pour apprédre à parler : qui n'est
chose moderne : car Pline au chapitre quarante-deuxiesme du dixiesme liure de
l'histoire naturelle,dit,que de long téps les fils de l'Empereur auoyent vn Estout-

Psaroi en Grec,Sturnus en Latin,Estourneau en François

j & ψάρες ὑψι πικκόμε,ψιφόσε δ' ὑψι ὀλίγον κόνιφρο. Arist.lib.9.cap.15.

neau qui parloit Grec, & Latin. Il est de couleur changeante, de mesme le collier   *Descrip-*
d'vn Ramiër, & madré de merques tannees par tout le corps, meslees de gris, &   *tion de*
de cendré, semees seulement sur le bout des plumes : lesquelles ne sont commu-   *l'Estour-*
nement comme celles des autres oyseaux, d'autant qu'elles sont plus estroictes   *neau.*
& longuettes,comme sont celles qu'on voit autour du col des Chapons. Et comme l'Oustarde, la Cane petiere, le Tercot, la Griue ont leurs taches diuersement
dessus les plumes, quasi depuis la racine : aussi l'Estourneau les à seulement mer-

---

fuscus, pars supina alba, maculis aliquot aspersa cinereis. partem etiam sub cauda albere puto, lon-
giores alarum pennæ nigricant.rostrum longiusculum modicè inflectitur. Sed cum de occultatio-
ne eius nihil cognorim,œnanthen esse non assero. Speciem eius in præcedente pagina adiecimus.

DE ONOCROTALO.

Icon hæc onocrotali est, cepti in Heluetia in locu prope Tugium,quem ipsi inspeximus.

Onocrotali caput, à pictura quodam olim nobis communicatum.

Onocrotali figura ex tabula Septen-
trionali Olai Magni.

A.

ANC auem à Latinis truonem appellari Verrius Flaccus scripsit : unde Cæcilius Comi-
cus(ut citat Festus)irridens quendam ob nasi magnitudinem dixerit : Proh dij immorta-
les,unde hic proreptio truo? Kaath Hebraicam uocé, rosp, interpretantur alij cuculum,
alij onocrotalum, pelecanum,mergulum,upupam:ut diximus supra in historia Mergi in
Ee 5

Romæ, ut uel coturnicibus nihilo rariores sint, Athenæus. Theophrastus tradit inuectitios esse in
Asia pauones, Plinius. Pauo ex Barbaris ad Græcos exportari esse dicitur, Aelianus. In India
omnium maximi qui ubiq̃ sunt pauones nascuntur, Aelianus. Pauonum greges agrestes trans-
marini esse dicuntur in insulis Sami in luco Iunonis, item in Planasia insula M. Pisonis, Varro.
Pauus è Samo præstantior est, Gellius lib.7. Paui Iunoni sacri sunt, ut scribit Menodotus Samius
in descriptione templi Samiæ Iunonis;& forte(inquit) in Samo primùm & nati & educati sunt, ac
inde in alia loca distributi,ut recitat Athenæus. Babylonii pauones plurimos colore uario distinctos nutrit, Diodorus:tanquam illic maior pulchriorq̃ eorum uarietas sit quàm alibi, ut Cælius ac-
cipit. Clemens in Pædagogo homines gulosos pauonē Medum celebrare scribit. Pauo auis
uaria est toto genere, Aristot. Colores(uarios) incipit fundere in trimatu, Plinius & Aelian. Pauonis pennæ magnum quidem ornamentum habent, sed is sine corpore existit, Aelian. Auis est
pulcherrima, & pulchritudinis studiosa, Author de nat.rerum. Pauoni natura formæ è uolucribus
dedit palmam, Varro. ¶ Pauonis apicem crinitæ arbusculæ cõstituunt, Plinius. Auis est paruo
capite, & quasi serpentino, & longis pennis coronato,russo, Albertus. Pluma ei in capite instar co-
ronæ uel potius cristæ,Author de nat.rerum. Collum longum,sapphiri colore, Idem & Albertus.
Pauonum ceruix,quoties aliquò deflectitur, nitet, Seneca lib.1.nat.quæst. Pectus quoque colore
sapphiri est,lucidum,alæ ruffæ : dorsum cinereum, ad ruborem declinans, Albertus. Pedes ssat,
Aristot. apud Athen. Aues non uolaces,ut pauones, gallinæ, uropygium (caudam pennis condi-
tam)ineptum habent,(non aptum flecti qua parte cum cute coalescit,) Aristot. Cauda pauoni ad
ornatum data est,Cicero,5.de finibus. Cauda mari est longa,pennis plumosa,& in fine pennarum
habet orbes ex uiridi quasi chrysolithi splendore, & auri & saphiri coloribus distinctos, Albertus.
Caudaq̃ pauonis larga cum luce repleta est, Consimili mutat ratione obuersa colores: Qui quo-
niam quodam gignuntur luminis ictu, Scire licet sine eo fieri non posse putandum,Lucret. lib.2.
Miraris quoties pennæ saeuo tradere duro coco,Martialis. Pa-
uonis caudæ pennarum oculos & gemmantes colores Plinius dixit, uide in D. Nullam autem pul-
chriorem pauone nostro fingere naturam posse credam, nisi cùm uidero, tot oculis in cauda tam
Gg 4

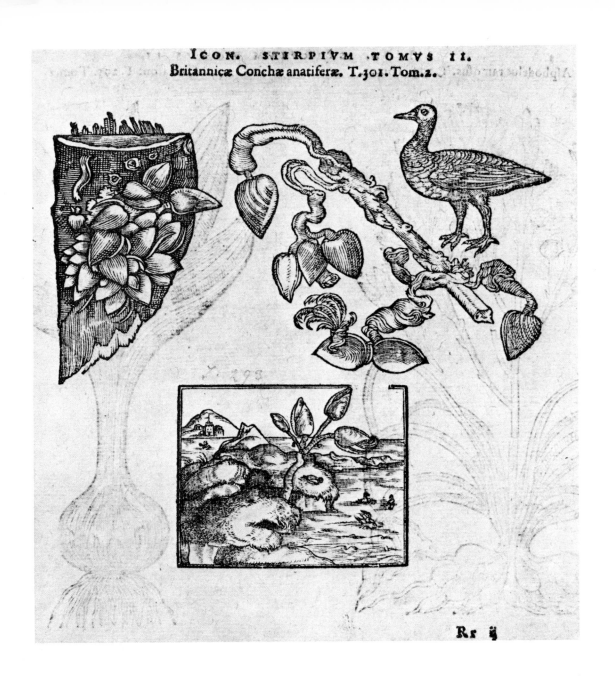

Rr ij

Concharum Anatiferarum , seu potius Ansiferarum variæ icones , necnon
& Berniclæ auis concharum earum vna enatæ effigies ponenda fol.174.

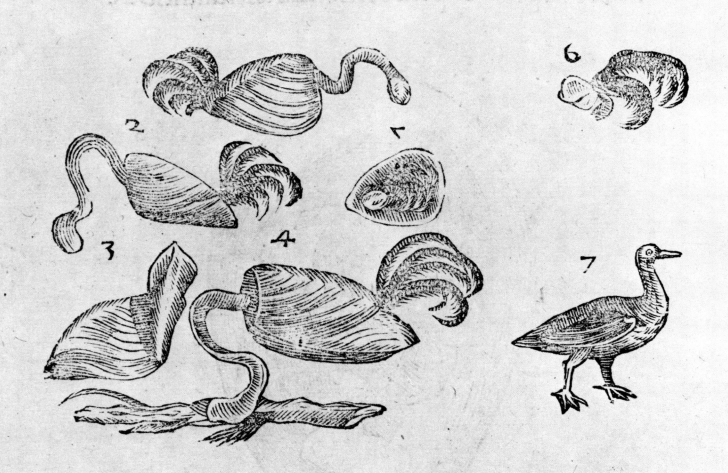

28, 29

Barnacle Goose *(Branta leucopsis)*

Plate 28 is from page 259 of *Icones Stirpium seu Plantarum tam exoticarum quam indigenarum . . .*, by Christopher Plantin, tom. II, Antwerp, 1591. Plate 29 is from page 548 of *Ornithologiae Tomus Tertius ac Postremus*, by Ulisse Aldrovandi, Bologna, 1639

The myth that Barnacle Geese were generated from *Lepas*, the Ship's Barnacle, was discussed in the Introduction to this book (pp. 11–12). Plantin's illustrations were based on earlier work by l'Obel. (The inset in Plate 28 is derived from page 655 of *Plantarum seu Stirpium Historia*, by Matthias de l'Obel, Antwerp, 1576.) Aldrovandi published his plate, which was taken from various sources, in the first edition of his *Ornithologiae*, 1599, which appeared during his lifetime. He had his doubts about the whole matter but remarked that since it had been vouched for by so many others, it was possible that there was something in it.

Woodcuts, 7 × 8·3 in. (178 × 208 mm.) and 5·5 × 7 in. (139 × 177 mm.)

30

Paduan Cock *(Gallus* sp.*)*

Plate CCIX from *Ornithologia Methodice Digesta . . . Illuminatis Ornata*,
by Xaverio Manetti, Vol. 2, Florence, 1767–76

This portrait of a Paduan cock possesses the flamboyant quality which
is typical of Manetti's illustrations (see Plate 85) and which in this
case is so aptly applied to a domesticated bird that in its various forms has
always been attractive to artists. Even in recent decades Picasso and
Lurçat have found something fresh to state about these birds.

Engraving and watercolour, 13·75 × 10·1 in. (349 × 255 mm.)

31, 32, 33, 34
OVERLEAF

Ruff *(Philomachus pugnax)*

Plate 31 from a German broadsheet, *Ein Warhafftige beschreibung . . .*,
Nuremberg, 1587; Plate 32 from a German booklet, *Der 7 Vögel
warhafftige Contrafectura*, Augsburg, 1587; Plates 33 and 34 from pages
418 and 420 of *Ornithologiae hoc est de Avibus historiae Libri XII*, by
Ulisse Aldrovandi, Bologna, 1637–46 (first edition 1599)

The part played by Conrad Gesner (1516–65) and Ulisse Aldrovandi
(1522–1605) in organizing sixteenth-century knowledge of the various
branches of zoology into encyclopedic natural histories has been discussed
elsewhere in this volume (pp. 19–20). Aldrovandi in particular amassed
great natural history collections and employed artists to paint them, such
as Cornelius Sivint from Frankfurt, Lorenzo Bernini from Florence and
Coriolanus of Nuremberg. His engravings of seven different types of
ruffs in breeding plumage were not Belgian in origin, as he states, but
were based on paintings by an English artist working in York. This is
made explicit by two German publications of 1587 to which my attention
was drawn by Mr Dennis Paisey of the British Library. The ruffs were
shot at Crowley near Hatfield on the Yorkshire-Lincolnshire border on
27 December 1586 and described by Richard Waller and Richard
Preston; the paintings were printed in London by Robin or Robinson
(whose name does not appear in the catalogue of early English printers),
and copied in the Netherlands, Nuremberg and Augsburg. The names
of the reliable English witnesses who testified to have seen the birds alive
and dead may be seen at the bottom of the Nuremberg broadsheet
(Plate 31). These publications have a special interest in that they suggest
how widely the knowledge of natural history was being diffused outside
the universities.

The Augsburg woodcut must have created an exceptional sensation;
another version, without the wondering boys, appeared as a French
watercolour of the seventeenth century, from the Bibliothèque Nationale,
in *L'Oiseau* (1963) by Simonne Jacquemard.

Plate 31, coloured woodcut, 6·3 × 4·7 in. (160 × 120 mm.); Plate 32,
coloured woodcut, detail from title page, 3 × 2·7 in. (75 × 70 mm.);
Plates 33 and 34, woodcuts, 13·75 × 9·25 in. (350 × 235 mm.) and 9 × 6 in.
(229 × 153 mm.)

Gallo Padovano. ━━━━━━━ Gallus Patavinus.

All'Ill:mo Sig:re Girolamo Benaßai Senatore, e Patrizio Lucchese.

Ein Warhafftige beschreibung vnd vrtheil von etlichen

Frembden vögeln/ der gleichen vor nie/ aber itzund in Engelandt/ in der Grafschafft von Licolne sind gesehen worden/ welche Federn an ihren hälsen/ vnd Stirnen sich den grossen Krössen oder auffgeribenen harlocken vergleichen wie gegenwertige Figur außweist.

ICh stelle Freundtlich Lieber leser dir hie ein Specktackel für die augen welchs mit dem Pensel des Mahlers oder mit der Feder auch von Plinio selbsten nicht so eigentlichen hette abgerissen können werden/ wie es wol die seltzamkeit erfodert/ vnnd es wirdig solches mit andacht zu hertzigen/ vnnd zu gemüet zu füeren/ Dann da der gleichen vor zeiten in Egypten/ Syrien/ Grecia/ Roma oder auch itzund bey den vnglaubigen Heyden gesehen worden/ hette solches einig Bedeutung jren warsagern Sternsehern/ Oraclen/ vnnd Altarn sonders zweiffel nicht wenig bekümmernuß vnd nachdencken gemacht. Wir aber oder Ja vil vnter vns sind in kurtz solche natürliche Philosophi worden/ in der gleichen wunderreichen (wan Ichs anderst so nenen mag) das wir/ dadurch vns selbsten/ auch vil andere der Natur erkundigung Liebhaber/ vnter den selben auch wol Weyse/ zu vnachtsamen Narren machen/ Weil wir vns vber dieselben nicht mit ehr erbietung verwundern/ Pharaonis Treum von Joseph selbsten außgelegt/ sindt Egypten vnd dem gantzen volck Israel nutzlich gewesen. Auch erschrack Balthasar nicht one vrsach/ da er die hand schreiben sahe/ ehe dan jm die schrifft durch Daniel erklert wurde/ wie dan gleichfals der Stern nicht ohn vrsach in Orient geschienen/ welchs die Weisen zu vnserm Seligmacher Christo gen Bethlehem beleytet/ vnd sind dergleichen Historien in weltlich Sachen vnzelich von Geistern vnuernünfftige thieren vögeln/ Wundergeburten begegnuß der Element/ Feuerflammen/ gesichten/ vund andern dingen/ die Ainigen Stenden/ oder Particular Personen gutes oder böses gedroet vns vor gedeutet/ oder (wie Mann sagt) auch ohne sprach/ offt Reformation vnd Besserung geprediget haben. Solches aber zuerzelen/ will Ich geliebtet/ kurtz halbn vmbgehen/ vnd eile zubeschreiben/ ein seltzam warhafftig auch Wunderlich/ vnd sehr Frembds geschicht/ so in Engeland vnlangst für gefallen/ vnd als Warhafftig von vilen Personen grosser Authoritet/ vnd Glaubwirdigkeit ist bezeuget worden/ wie hernach Volgt.

Es ist geschehen in dem 1586. Jar/ in der Pfarr von Crowlei so gelegen bey der Wisen/ der Herschafft von Hatfilde/ in der Grafschafft von Licolne das Einer mit Namen Richart Wallar/ vnd dan ein ander Reichat preston so auß derselben Pfarr Crowlei gewesen/ etliche Leim ruhten gestelt haben/ darmit sie gefangen vnd bekommen haben/ Sieben grosse Vögel/ alle in einerley grössen/ vnd von Vnterschiedlichen farben/ dergleichen keiner jemals gefunden/ auch dieselben oder jre Conterfeyung nie gesehen oder daruon gehört hat. Welche vögel nach dem Leben in jren warhafftigen farben durch deß Er: Herrn Heinrich Leo Maler vff begern deß Er: Herrn Heinrich Leo Ritter durch einen Maler in Yorcke abgerissen vnd etlichen hohen Personen vnterschiedlich außgetheilet sind worden. Vnd sind newlich Drey derselben dem vorgemelten Herren Heinrichen Leo verehrt/ vnd geschenckt worden/ welcher damals bey seinem Brudern zu Hatfilde/ in der Prouinz von Yorck logiret war. die federn auff jhren häuptern vnd Stirnen/ auß gebreitet/ wie das auffgeribene oder gebüste har/ an Männern vnd weibern vnd die Federn rings vmb Jre helse/ von Vnterschidenen farben/ so auß einander/ vnd hoch auffgericht stunden/ aller maß wie die grossen Kröß/ vnd waren vntersetzt mit einem Stenglin gleich als ob es Eiserner drath oder dergleichen vntersetzung were/ wie Jtzundt vnser hüebsche gesellen im brauch haben. Diese Vögel da sie loß vnd ledig daher gingen haben gleichsam jhre freyheit nichts geacht/ vnnd nit gesorgt wie sie Möchten dauon fliegen/ Also das sie durch Einiges trohen/ oder zu sammen schlagen/ der hende weder weichen/ noch Jemals haben scheuhe werden wöllen. Sonder sind stetigs in einer gestalt/ ohne wesen bliben. jr gebrauch war aller

drey in grosser Ordnung vff dem Saal auff vnd ab zugehen/ offt stil zu stehen/ vnd jhre Köpf vnd Schnebel zusammen zustecken/ als ob sie eine gute Weil/ gleichsam in einer Consultation/ oder einer wichtigen sache Raht hilten/ vnd als dan wider zugehen/ ohne einiges begern Jhrer Natur/ zu essen oder andere anreytzung zu nemen. Wie wol es jnen manichmal ward angebotten vnd in disem Stande sind sie verhart/ bis sie alle Drey/ einer nach dem andern dahin gestorben. Ohngefehr drey Tag nach dem sie Gefangen worden/ Nach dem sie Todt waren/ konte Niemandt mit beyden Henden eine einige jrer Federn/ Vmb den halß bewegen/ oder Verrücken. Man hat etliche Vögelsteller erfordert vnd sie dieselben sehen lassen/ hat aber von jhnen nichts erfaren können/ von was art Vögeln sie gewesen/ noch vil weniger/ daß sie dergleichen gesehen/ oder Jemals dauon gehört hetten.

Was dieses für Vögel gewesen/ auß Was vrsach sie Herwerts geflogen/ vnd alhie gefangen sind/ Item was jhre Eigenschafft/ vnd jhre hieuor erzehlte Farben bedeuten mögen/ ist mir Vnbewüst/ Allein mercke ich diß/ das das jenige/ so bey disen Vögeln vber Natürlich scheint zu sein/ auch in anschauung vnser Kleydung vnd Schmuck vberflüssig bey vns Gebraucht Wird. Es were meines bedünckens/ ein glücklich oder leydliche Jrtung (da es anderst eine Jrtung wer) wan es vnsere Edle frawen vnd Junckfrawen/ so mit auffgeribenem haar/ vü Langen Krössen daher brangen/ da für hilten/ daß diese art/ der Vögel auffgeribene vnd gekröste Teuffel weren gewesen.

Wolte Gott/ daß solche wunder Vögel etlichen so zu grossen Krössen lust haben/ ein anen vnd vber zeugen möchten/ das sie selbst solche monstra vnd vngeheure Menschen weren/ Laßt vns auch Endlich betrachten/ das vns vnser Schöpffer nit geschaffen hat das wir vns also soln verstellen/ vü vermummen/ weil wir zu seinem eignem Ebenbildt erschaffen sindt. Ein wenig Kleider befridiget vnd stillet die Natur/ vnd alles was vber Flüssig/ vnd zu vil ist/ das ist böch vnnd schedlich/ Nackend sind wir in diese Welt geborn/ Nackendt solln wir wider begraben werden/ vnd damals war der mensch eigentlich glückselig da er gantz Nackent lebete/ Solte derhalben das anschauen der Kleidung vns abwenden von allem pracht vnd Hoffart/ vnd vns erinnern Darbey zu Bedencken daß sie nur eine bedeckung seyen vnserer Scham/ vnd ein Elende Merckzeichen Adams vbertretung vnd Vnserer Erbsünde/ sollen also gleich dem Schwan durch das anschauen vnserer Schwartzen füß/ vnsere eitele. vü Hoffertige Kleydung weg werffen/ vnd gedencken/ das der aller schöneste nit sey wie ein Blume/ vnd der so am lengsten Lebet/ doch entlich Sterben muß/ das auch diese leibliche Creatur/ gleich einem Schrecken todten Leychnam darnider ligen/ vnd vnsere Geschmückte leiber stinckende Wurm aß werden Sollen.

Damit ich mich aber nit vil mehr zu Predigen das ich nit kan Vnterstehe/ als ein Prodigium oder Wunderzeichen dafür ichs hab zu erschelen/ So beschliesse ich. Es sey gleich dem Glaubigen oder Vnglaubigen Leser mit diesem Monstro gedienet oder nit gedienet/ das es dannoch vil Seltzamer vnd Wunderlicher/ dan es hie abgerissen vnd beschrieben ist/ vnd bin deßen gewiß das der augen mehr sind die dasselbe gesehen vnd bezeugen können Dan daß Einiger zweyffel/ oder Cauilation das widerlegen könte/ oder Ich Ainiger mühe bedürffen solte/ Solches zu versichern/ Gehabt euch woll vü Fliehet die Hoffart.

Penes Authorem sit fides,

Die Namen der vnterschidlichen Erbarn/ vnd glaubwirdigen Personen/ so die vorgemelte.

Vögel gesehen haben/ weil sie gelebt/ vnd nach dem sie Gestorben.

Wilhelm Boner/ ein Edelman erkleret diß warhafftig sein.

Thomas Mall. Balliëu von Hatfeldt.

Ambrosius Banckfore ein Edelman so damals

In H: Heinrich Leo dinsten/ bezeugen auch dasselbige.

Meister Thomas Richart.

Meister Simon Wormlei.

Meister Thomas Pamer/ mit etlich andern (mehr)

Gedruckt zu Nürnberg durch Georg Lanng Formschneider in der Jüden gassen.

cætera ſimilis ſit, ſubnectere placuit. Equidem natura luſiſſe videtur in eius generatione
auritam faciens, cùm ex nullis diurnis aliam inuenias. Roſtro eſt, vt aues pugnaces gracili,
& oblongo, oblongis etiam alis. A capite per collum pennæ vndiquaque pendent magni-
tudine a quales, ſed in quibus varios cernere eſt colores, qui velut varios torques formant,
modò ferrugineos, modò rubros, modò albos. Aures longæ ſunt aſininis non diſſimiles.
Longum item collũ eſt, & valde gracile, atque tenue, ad latera candicans, cætero luteſcens,
lineolis nigris vndiquaque conſperſum. Roſtrum, caput, alæ, aures, & dorſum coloris ſunt
ferruginei. Venter, femora, quæ ad genua vſque pennis veſtiuntur, luteſcent. Tibia, & pe-
dum digiti coloris, ferè carnei. Digitus poſticus admodum breuis. Caput ad latera minia-
ceam maculam magnam habet, in qua oculi ſiti ſunt: palpebræ oblongæ, inſignes, iris alba, pupilla nigra.

Auis pugnax ſeptima.

Acer rubrum.
Sp. pl. 2. 1496.

T. 62

Parus &c.

Acer &c

35
Yellow-throated Warbler *(Dendroica dominica)*

Plate 62 from *The Natural History of Carolina . . .*, by Mark Catesby,
Vol. I, London, 1731–43

Although there had been other naturalists in North America before
Mark Catesby, he was the first to make comprehensive collections of birds
and to publish detailed notes and descriptions of them. He is therefore
rightly regarded as the father of American ornithology. He was, however,
English by birth, and his family lived at Castle Hedingham in Essex; the
family house, where he was born in 1682, is still standing. His boyhood
interests were in natural history; when a young man he moved to London
in order to meet people with similar tastes. He first visited America in
1712, probably to see his sister Elizabeth, who had married Dr William
Cocke, Secretary of State in Virginia, and on this visit he sent some plants
to the Chelsea Physic Garden, the oldest botanic garden in England,
founded in 1673 by the Society of the Art and Mistery of Apothecaries
of the City of London. In 1712 the garden was acquired by Sir Hans
Sloane who returned it to the Society a few years later by a deed of
conveyance. In 1715 Catesby visited Jamaica, where Sloane had been
appointed physician to the Duke and Duchess of Albemarle in 1707.
Owing to the Duke's death Sloane had less time there than he had hoped
but that visit probably served as an early link with Catesby. In 1719 there
was a plan to send a collector to Africa; both Albin (Plate 23) and Catesby
were possible candidates but finally Catesby abandoned the idea and
began instead to make plans to return to North America. With the
patronage of William Sherard (a well-known botanist who founded the
Chair of Botany in Oxford), Sir Hans Sloane and other scientists,
subscriptions were raised and Catesby finally sailed in April 1722. He was
commissioned primarily as a botanist and he had to work very hard
indeed to find the time for work on the birds which he had begun to
draw on his first visit.

Like Eleazar Albin (p. 21), Catesby taught himself to draw, engrave
and colour his own plates. His two-volume work on the natural history
of Carolina contains over one hundred plates of birds with plants on
which they feed or with which they are associated in some way or other.
Furthermore it was published with the text in parallel columns of French
and English.

Catesby wrote that this little warbler 'weighs seven Penny-weight . . .
The Feet are brown; and like those of the *Certhia* have very long Claws,
which assist them in creeping about Trees in search of Insects, on which
they feed. There is neither Black nor Yellow upon the Hen. They are
frequent in Carolina.'

Engraving, 14 × 10 in. (355 × 260 mm.)

36, 37, 38, 39, 40, 41, 42, 43
Various birds

Plates from *Historia de Gentibus Septentrionalibus . . .*, by Olaus Magnus, Rome, 1555: Plate 36, *De Ciconiis* [storks], p. 658; Plate 37, *De Hirundinibus ab aquis extractis* [swallows taken from the water], p. 673; Plate 38, *De Columbarum genere, & colorum varietate.* [kinds of pigeons and their colour forms], p. 662; Plate 39, *De nivalibus Aviculis* [small birds' nests], p. 679; Plate 40, *De Avibus nocturnis, & earum cibis* [nocturnal birds and their food], p. 692; Plate 41, *De Ovis insularibus diversarum avium* [eggs of various birds on islands], p. 681; Plate 42, *De diversis Avibus natura contrarius* [various birds with unusual natures], p. 688; Plate 43, *De Perdicibus, & venatione earum* [partridges and how they are caught], p. 685

Olaus Magnus (1490–1557), Archbishop of Uppsala and Metropolitan of Sweden, fled from his country during the Reformation and lived in exile in Danzig and Italy for much of his life. His account of the northern peoples was published in Rome and, presumably, all the illustrations are by an Italian artist. Although he was credulous and upheld various myths such as that of the Barnacle Goose (Plates 28 and 29 and p. 11) his work is valuable in being the first published account of Scandinavia and because he foreshadows the ecological treatment of birds.

One of his most famous plates shows two fishermen hauling up a net wherein the fishes lie side by side with swallows, of which he observes:

> Though many Writers of Natural Histories have written that Swallows change their stations, that is when cold Winter begins to come, they fly to hotter Climats; yet, oft-times in the Northern Countries, Swallows are drawn forth, by chance, by Fishermen, like a lump cleaving together, where they went amongst the Reeds, after the beginning of Autumn, and there fasten themselves bill to bill, wing to wing, feet to feet. For it is observed, that they, about that time, ending their most sweet note do so descent, and they fly out peaceably after the beginning of spring.

The belief that swallows hibernated persisted long after Adanson found them overwintering in Senegal although his account of his travels there, from 1749 to 1753, was published within a few years of his return. It was partly an emotional issue and people who knew little or nothing about natural history took sides. Even Dr Johnson gave his verdict: 'Swallows certainly sleep all winter. A number of them conglobulate together by flying round and round, and then all in a heap throw themselves under water, and lye in the bed of a river.'

As late as 1882 a formal article appeared in *Hardwicke's Science Gossip* reviewing many statements of supposedly reputable persons, who claimed to have seen swallows resuscitated after prolonged immersion, showing how these beliefs had grown and how they could not be true.

Woodcuts, each approximately 2·3 × 4·7 in. (59 × 122 mm.)

DE AVIBVS.

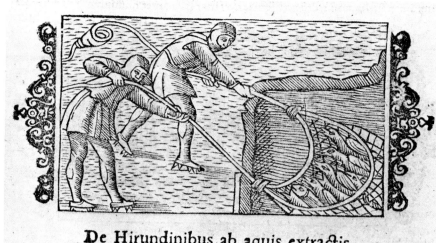

De Ciconiis.

De Hirundinibus ab aquis extractis.

DE AVIBVS.

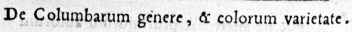

De Columbarum genere, & colorum varietate.

LIBER XIX.

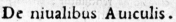

De niualibus Auiculis.

DE AVIBVS.

De Auibus nocturnis, & earum cibis.

LIBER XIX.

De Ouis insularibus diuersarum auium.

DE AVIBVS.

De diuersis Auibus natura contrariis.

LIBER XIX.

De Perdicibus, & venatione earum.

CREVIT IN NIDOS

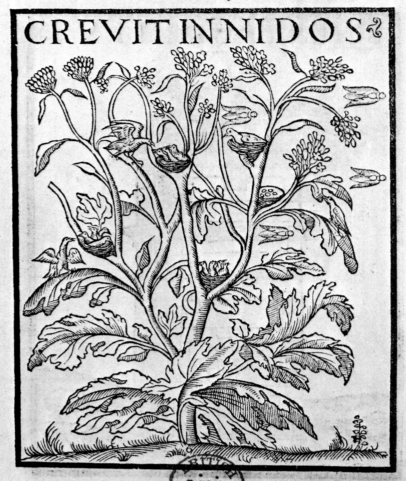

Quod cadit in terram neglectum ex arbore granum,
    Consequitur casu commoda magna suo.
Paulatim crescit, distendit in æthera ramos,
    Miratur fructus, & sua poma timet.
At postquam iustam compleuit caudice formam,
    Vmbra viris grata est, altibus'q; domus.

SCIENTIAM FILI VS

Candida fertur auis, terror, pestis'q; colubris,
    Quæ nutrit patris tempora sera sui:
Te puerum musæ lactarunt, præmia poscunt,
    Implorat prolem docta Minerua suam.

H ij

44, 45
Various birds (stylized)
Storks *(Ciconia ciconia)*

Plates on pages 116 and 115 of *Publica Laetitia . . .*, edited by Alvarez
Gomez de Castro, Compluti, ?1546

The woodcuts in this sixteenth-century Spanish work have considerable
charm but the meaning of the emblems is obscure as the Latin is
colloquial. The lines referring to the storks are written in a Latin so
corrupt that they seem untranslatable.

The first verse might be considered to be an archaic version of the
slogan *Plant a tree in 1973*; more precisely it may be rendered:

The seed which falls to the ground from the tree, unnoticed,
Is followed by great profit from its fall :
Slowly it grows, stretching its branches to the sky,
It wonders at its produce and fears for its fruit,
But when its trunk has grown to its full size,
Its shade is welcome to men and to the high nests.

Woodcuts, 4·85 × 3·7 in. (124 × 94 mm.) and 4·9 × 3·9 in. (125 × 100 mm.)

46

Prairie Chicken *(Tympanuchus cupido)*

Plate 1 from the Appendix to *The Natural History of Carolina . . .*, by
Mark Catesby, Vol. II, London, 1731–43

In this plate Catesby has taken as much trouble with his painting of
Dodecatheon, a member of the Primulaceae, as with his Prairie Chicken.
Dodecatheon is a genus confined to North America; some of the species
make choice garden plants, and have the same kind of charm as the
European *Cyclamen* which are also members of the Primulaceae though
not as closely related to the American genus as their reflexed petals suggest.

   Tympanuchus is a bird of the grasslands and prairies but *Dodecatheon*
is more likely to be found in woodlands, especially in mountainous areas
of the west. See also Plate 35.

Engraving, 14 × 10·2 in. (355 × 265 mm.)

47

Toco Toucan *(Ramphastos toco)*

Plate on page 802 of *Ornithologiae hoc est de Avibus historiae Libri XII,*
by Ulisse Aldrovandi, Bologna, 1637 (first edition 1599)

Aldrovandi (1522–1605) was born at Bologna and ultimately became a
professor there. He was exceedingly industrious and prepared an
encyclopedic work on natural history, but only four of the volumes—
those on birds and insects—were published during his lifetime. He was
less critical than Gesner (p. 19) but his range was greater and the
illustrations to his books were prepared by trained artists; he was more
interested than Gesner in anatomy and he included accounts of a greater
number of exotic species.

The first account of toucans to appear in Europe was apparently one
by Oviedo in his *Oviedo : de la natural hystoria de las Indias* (1526).
Toucans are confined to the tropical regions of the Americas; their striking
plumage attracted the attention of the early European explorers,
particularly since their beaks and feathers were used for decorative
purposes by the natives. Aldrovandi's plate is based on one by Gesner,
but he does not acknowledge this although he sometimes gives his
sources (see Plates 33, 34).

Toucans breed in holes or hollows in trees. Most of them take no
lining into their nests but the floor becomes covered with the hard seeds
regurgitated from the fruit on which they largely feed; this forms a layer
which must feel very much like pebbles to the naked young. The
nestlings, however, possess thickened heel pads from which rings of
prominent tubercles project which serve to keep them from being damaged
by the seeds. Toucans sleep with the tail lying flat along the back and the
great bill pointing backwards in a similar position. Although the woodcut
reproduced here suggests that the beak is out of proportion, this is not
so; in some species it is actually as long as the rest of the body. It is
quite light; internally there are many air spaces in a fibrous network.
Humboldt and Bonpland (see Plate 87) carried one of these birds as a pet
in their canoe on the Orinoco.

Woodcut, 13 × 8·5 in. (330 × 216 mm.)

48
Skeletons of man and bird
Plates on pages 40 and 41 of *L'Histoire de la nature des Oyseaux . . .*,
by Pierre Belon, Paris, 1555

Belon's position in the development of zoological science, and more
particularly ornithology and ichthyology, has been discussed in the
Introduction (see p. 19 and Plates 24 and 25). This plate shows the first
attempt to homologize the human and avian skeleton by means of
illustrations; it is thus a milestone in the history of comparative anatomy.

Woodcuts, 13 × 8 in. (330 × 203 mm.)

Portraict de l'amas des os humains, mis en comparaison de l'anatomie de ceux des oyseaux, faisant que les lettres d'icelle se raporteront à ceste cy, pour faire apparoistre combien l'affinité est grande des vns aux autres.

La comparaison du susdit portraict des os humains monstre combien cestuy cy qui est d'vn oyseau, en est prochain.

Portraict des os de l'oyseau.

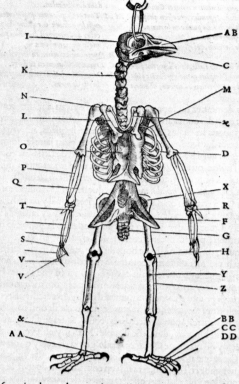

A B Les Oyseaux n'ont dents ne leures, mais ont le bec tranchant fort ou foible, plus ou moins selon l'affaire qu'ils ont eu à mettre en pieces ce dont ils viuent.

M Deux pallerons longs & estroicts, vn en chascun costé.

æ L'os qu'on nommé la Lunette ou Fourchette n'est trouué en aucun autre animal, hors mis en l'oyseau.

D Six costes, attachees au coffre de l'estomach par deuãt, & aux six vertebres du dos par derriere.

F Les deux os des hanches sont longs, car il n'y a aucunes vertebres au dessoubs des costes.

G Six osselets au cropion.

H La rouelle du genoil.

I Les sutures du test n'apparoissent gueres sinon qu'il soit boully.

k Douze vertebres au col, & six au dos.

Le Faucon Pélerin femelle? Accipiter Peregrinus faemina. Sparviere Pellegrino femina.

Maddalena Bouchard

49

Peregrine Falcon *(Falco peregrinus)*

Plate from *Recueil de Cent-Trente-trois Oiseaux des plus belles Espèces . . .*,
by Maddalena Bouchard, Rome, 1775

Madame Bouchard based this highly coloured work on copies from
Manetti's *Ornithologia Methodice Digesta* (Plates 30, 85) although she failed
to acknowledge her source. She embellished the originals with the most
improbable additions, owing something perhaps to some of the more
exaggerated plates by Maria Sybille Merian (Plate 1). The drawings are
full of vitality and comic touches and make one feel that the unscrupulous
author must have been a most entertaining person.

Peregrines have a world-wide distribution and have been used by
falconers in all countries where hawking is practised. In the air they are
the most brilliant of performers, and hunt with a dash and precision that
is unmatched. Peregrines usually kill in full flight the birds on which they
prey; they also feed on small vertebrates, and even beetle remains have
been found at their eyries, so that it is possible that the presence of the
grasshopper in this plate is less far-fetched than it appears.

Engraving, 15·1 × 12·55 in. (385 × 320 mm.)

50

Eagles, various

Plate 1 from *Ornithologiae hoc est de Avibus historiae Libri XII* by Ulisse Aldrovandi, Frankfurt, 1610

This composite plate shows Aldrovandi's general approach to natural history (see pp. 19, 20 and Plates 33, 34, 51) which included classical and mythological sources; it also suggests his own interest in anatomy which probably owed something to both Belon (p. 19) and Coeiter (Plate 22). The etching of the Golden Eagle in the top right-hand corner was used in a larger mirror version in the original and other editions of this work (Plate 51).

Etching, 14 × 8·3 in. (355 × 210 mm.)

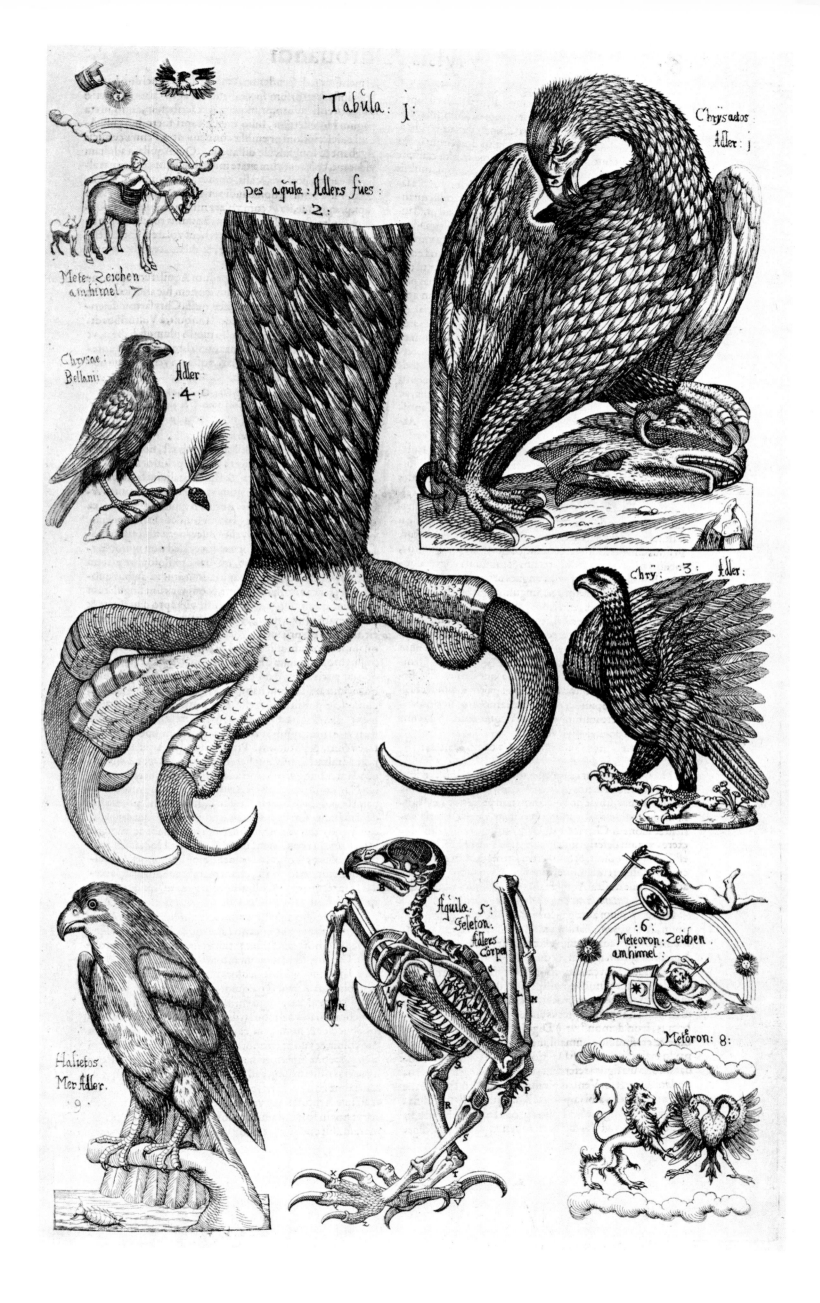

Tabula: I.

pes aquile: Adlers fues
: 2 .

Chrysaetos
Adler: 1.

Chrysae
Bellanii
Adler
: 4 .

Meter Zeichen
amhimel 7.

Chry: 3: Adler:

Aquila: 5:
Seleton:
Adlers
Corper:

: 6 .
Meteoron Zeichen
amhimel:

Meteoron: 8:

Halietos.
Mer Adler.
: 9 .

K 2

51

Golden Eagle *(Aquila chrysaëtos)*

Plate facing page 110 of *Ornithologiae hoc est de Avibus historiae Libri XII*, by Ulisse Aldrovandi, Bologna, 1646 (first edition 1599)

One would like to know who executed the original drawing from which this plate was engraved. It was much copied and rightly so since it shows great mastery of the technique of wood engraving. See also Plate 50 for a smaller version of the same subject, and for a more detailed reference to Aldrovandi see Plates 31–34.

Wood engraving, 12 × 7·4 in. (305 × 185 mm.)

52

Lapwing *(Vanellus vanellus)*

Plate XI from *A Natural History of British Birds etc . . .*, by William
Hayes, London, 1775

William Hayes was an industrious character of no great originality whose
plates of birds vary in quality; some are believed to have been executed
by himself, others by members of his very large family—he is said to have
had twenty-one children. Although this engraving of the lapwing fails
to convey its rich colouring seen at close quarters, it has a charm of its
own. Flocks of lapwings, especially in Ireland where they may consist
of very large numbers, have a unique leisurely quality when they are
seen flying against a wintry sky.

Engraving, 16·5 × 12 in. (429 × 310 mm.)

53, 54
OVERLEAF

Various Owls

Plates XVIII and XIX from *Historiae Naturalis de Avibus*, by Joannes
Jonstonius, Amsterdam, 1657 (first edition 1650–55)

Jonston was Scottish by birth but lived abroad most of his life; he is
sometimes called John Johnston but here he is given the name that
appears on the title page of his best-known work on birds. It is largely a
compilation from Gesner and Aldrovandi but contains useful references
to works from the time of Aristotle and Pliny onwards. These references
are well arranged. It was only in the later editions that the engraver is
named; a century after the first edition appeared one was published in
Heilbron with a much more elaborate title:

> *Theatrum universale de Avibus tabulis duabus et sexaginta ab illo*
> *celeberrimo Mathias Meriano aeri incisi ornatum ex scriptoribus tam*
> *antiquis quam recentioribus, Theophrasto, Dioscoride, Aeliano, Oppiano,*
> *Plinio, Gesnero, Aldrovandro . . . Marggravio, Pisone . . .*

The engraver was either the father or the brother of Maria Sybille
Merian, the painter of the Muscovy Duck that is the subject of the first
plate in this volume.

Engravings, each 11·5 × 7·2 in. (292 × 182 mm.)

Plate XI.

Wm Hayes Del.^t   Gabr.^l Smith Sculp.^t

Tab XVIII

Bubo   Nacht Eule

Bubo

Bubo Berghu Hutu
hiwu

Ulula Eule

Bubo Kautz   Aietz

Asio
buhonus Species

Asio alius seu Scops

Asio seu Otus Ohrul

Ulula Kirch Eule

Tab. XIX

Ulula Uwel

Ulula

Hubu eule

Aluco maßnw

Noctua

Strix

Noctua

Saxatils

Noctua

Kauzlein

Steinkauz

Ulula alia

Tab. XXXIII.

Die Blau-Meise in zweyen Vorstellungen.

Das Scelet obigen Vogels auf zweyerley Art.

J. D. Meyer ad viv. fec. et exc. Norimb.

55

Blue Tits *(Parus caeruleus)*

Plate 33 from *Angenehmer und nützlicher Zeit-Vertreib mit Betrachtung . . .*,
by J. D. Meyer, Nuremberg, 1748–56

J. D. Meyer (1713–52) was a professional miniature painter who set to
work to draw as many mammals and birds as he could. He is an aberrant
figure in the history of ornithology, since he had a morbid interest in
depicting monsters and deformities with baroque backgrounds; some of
this feeling is apparent in the unnatural attitudes of the skeletons which
appear in most of his paintings of animals. Even in his paintings of human
beings or mythological subjects he liked to have a symbol of death in a
prominent position. His contribution to the development of ornithological
illustration is slight, although his work has achieved a certain degree of
popularity. His work has been briefly discussed in recent years by Gunter
Mann in an essay *Medizinisch-naturwissenschaftliche Buchillustration im
18. Jahrhundert in Deutschland*, 1964.

Engraving, 12·25 × 8·3 in. (312 × 210 mm.)

56
Various birds

Plate 56 from *Historiae Naturalis de Avibus*, by Joannes Jonstonius, Amsterdam, 1657

Jonston's claim to have included many exotic birds in his *Historiae* (Plates 53, 54) is implemented by some of those depicted in this plate. One of the toucans at the top of the page is identical with the species figured by Aldrovandi (Plate 47), the other cannot be identified precisely. The Portuguese gave the name Emu to the large ratite birds they discovered both in the new and old worlds. As a result, Clusius (see below) described a cassowary from the Moluccas as an *Emeu*, while Nieremberg (*c.* 1595–1658), a Spanish Jesuit naturalist, whose writings were based on those of Hernández (p. 19), called the South American Rhea an emu. The Australian species to which the name is exclusively applied today was not discovered until the late eighteenth century.

In the next row there is a Black-throated Diver on the left, a penguin from the Strait of Magellan in the centre, and on the right a bird instantly recognizable as an impoverished ancestor of Tenniel's Dodo in *Alice in Wonderland*. There used to be confusion between the northern auks and the southern penguins. (The French word for auk is *pingouin*, for penguin, *manchot*.) Accordingly Jonston's penguin from Tierra del Fuego has been endowed with the bill of a Great Auk, another flightless bird (see Plates 95, 96); both have an upright stance and are, and were, wonderful swimmers. At the bottom is a skua, a word derived from Skúir. This was the term used by a certain Hoier who about 1604 sent one of these birds from the Faroes to Charles LeCluse (Clusius) (1526–1609), a French naturalist and physician, from whom Willughby copied it. It has persisted as the British name for these birds. To the right of the skua is a humming-bird which Nieremberg called by the Brazilian name of Ourissia. The second name, Tominaeio, is derived from the Spanish word *tomin*, the weight of a third part of a drachm, hence generally used for any minute object.

It will be obvious that Jonston was an enthusiastic borrower but, since he gives his sources so conscientiously, he is most useful.

Engraving, 11·5 × 7·2 in. (292 × 182 mm.)

Pua Brasi.
alia

Altera Xochi
Tenacatl

Tab. 56

Pica Brasilica Toucan
Xochitenacatl

Emeu Clus

Emeu Nierenberg

Anser Magella:
nicus

Mergus arti:
§ Clus

Gall. peregrin.
Clu:

Cijgn. Cuculat
Nierenberg

Skua   Hoieri

Ourissia S. Tominio Niernb.

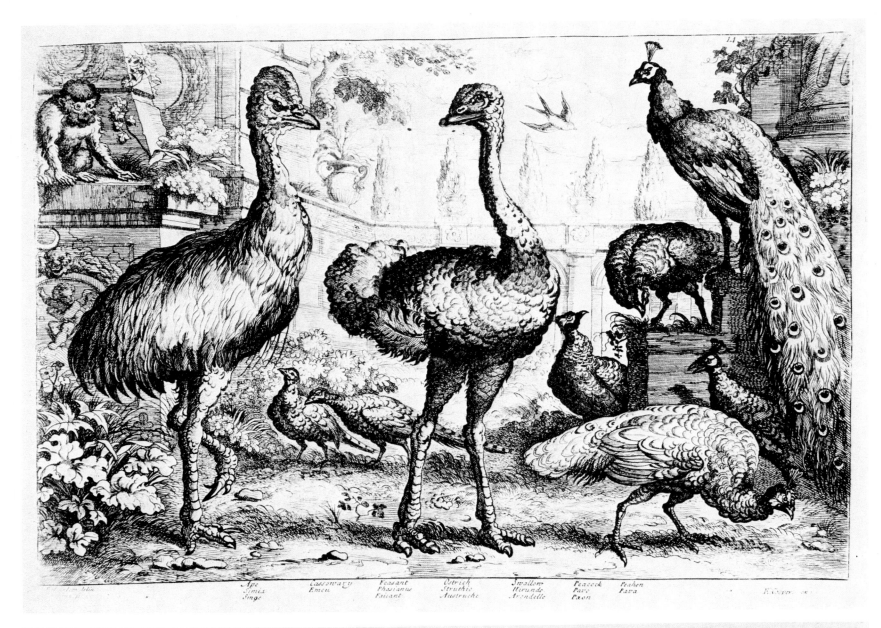

Ape	Cassowary	Feasant	Ostrich	Swallow	Peacock	Peahen	
Simia	Emeu	Phasianus	Struthio	Hirundo	Pavo	Pava	
Singe		Faisant	Austruche	Arondelle	Paon		F. Cooper ex.

Teal	Duck	Feasant	Hawke	Cormorant	Bittour	Owle	
Boscha	Anas domestica	Phasianus	Accipiter	Corvus Aquaticus	Butio	Bubo	
Sarcelle	cane		Espreuier			Hulotte	F. Cooper ex.

F. Barlow delin:
Scriptor fecit

57, 58
Various birds

Plates 13 and 11 from *Barlow's Birds and Beasts in Sixty-seven Excellent and Useful Prints . . .*, by Francis Barlow, London, 1775 (first edition 1655)

Barlow (1626–1702) was a professional artist with a particular gift for drawing birds. He is important in the development of sporting pictures in that he had an ability to see the landscape as an integral part of his design, and was therefore partly responsible for the notable development of this type of painting in the eighteenth century.

He prepared some of his own engravings but most of those in this series are by Wenceslaus Hollar. Some of these studies served as a basis for large oil paintings; thus there are matching oils of the cassowary and ostrich, full size, still to be seen at Clandon Park in Surrey.

Engravings, each 8·15 × 11·75 in. (213 × 302 mm.)

59
Stork *(Ciconia ciconia)*

Plate 24 from Vol. 3 of the Wellesley Collection, *c.* 1800, India Office Library, London

This is one of a series of 2,660 drawings of natural history subjects commissioned or collected by Richard Colley Wellesley (1760–1842), the first Marquis Wellesley, Governor-General of India 1797–1802.

Wellesley, whose younger brother Arthur was to become Duke of Wellington, was a first-class administrator, a gifted soldier and a man of great wisdom and integrity. He realized that the British would be unable to rule India successfully unless the civil servants became familiar with the languages, history and customs of the varied people who composed the population of the subcontinent. Accordingly he tried to set up colleges for men who intended to enter the service. This resulted in the establishment of Fort William College and then, in 1804, of the Institution for Promoting the Natural History of India, with a menagerie and aviary at Barrackpore.

In a memorandum to the Governors of the East India Company Wellesley wrote: 'The illustration and improvement of that important branch of the natural history of India, which embraces an object so extensive as the description of the principal parts of the animal kingdom, is worthy of the munificence and liberality of the English East India Company, and must necessarily prove an acceptable service to the world.' The Governors thought his plans too grandiose but eventually a college was set up in England, which later became Haileybury School. It was there that Webb-Smith (Plates 125, 126) and B. H. Hodgson (Plates 111, 140) were educated. The stimulus provided by such early training can be estimated by the great collections of natural history drawings, many by Indian artists, that were produced in the nineteenth century.

This drawing, by one of these unknown Indians, combines an accurately depicted bird against a typically Indian miniature landscape.

Watercolour, 15·75 × 8·6 in. (400 × 220 mm.)

24,

Samcool
Ardea Ciconia

LE GEANT.

LE SOLITAIRE

60, 61

White Dodo or Solitaire of Réunion Island
(Raphus solitarius)
Solitaire of Rodriguez Island (Pezophaps solitarius)

Plates facing page 72 of Vol. 2, and page 98 of Vol. 1, from
Voyage et avantures . . ., by F. Leguat, London, 1708

Leguat and his companions were Huguenot refugees who settled on
Rodriguez Island in 1691; they visited Réunion and also Mauritius where
the Dodo *(Raphus cucullatus)* may still have been in existence, though all
three species of these curious birds (believed to be aberrant members of
the pigeon family and confined to the Mascarene Islands) rapidly became
extinct after the arrival of European man with his pigs and rats.

Leguat wrote passionately about his exile, and there was originally
some doubt whether his account of the natural history of the islands was
authentic but the veracity of his descriptions has been largely vindicated
by the discovery of abundant fossil material. The following notes on the
Solitaire of Rodriguez are taken from the English translation:

Of all the Birds in the Island, the most Remarkable is that which goes
by the Name of the Solitary, because 'tis very seldom seen in Company,
tho' there are abundance of them . . . They have scarce any Tail, but
their Hind-part cover'd with Feathers is Roundish, like the Crupper of
a Horse, they are taller than Turkeys. Their Neck is straight, and a
little longer in proportion than a Turkeys, when it lifts up his Head.
Its Eye is black and lively and its Head without Comb or Cop. They
never fly, their Wings are too little to support the weight of their
Bodies; they serve only to beat themselves, and flutter when they call
one another. They will whirl about for twenty or thirty minutes
together on the same side, during the space of four or five Minutes. The
Motions of their Wings makes then a noise very like that of a Rattle and
one may hear it two hundred Paces off . . . The Females are
wonderfully beautiful, some fair, some brown; I call them fair because
they are of the colour of fair Hair . . . No one Feather is stragling from
the other all over their Bodies, they being very careful to adjust
themselves and make them all even with their Beak . . . They have two
Risings on their Craws, and the Feathers are whiter there than the rest
which livelily Represents the fine Neck of a Beautiful Woman. They
walk with so much Stateliness and good Grace, that one cannot help
admiring and loving them; by which means their fine Mein often saves
their Lives . . . After these Birds have rais'd their young One, and left it
to itself they are always together, which the other Birds are not, and
tho' they happen to mingle with other Birds of the same Species, these
two Companions never disunite . . . I admired the Happiness of these
innocent and faithful Pairs who liv'd so peacably in constant Love.

Engravings, each 5·3 × 3 in. (138 × 76 mm.)

62

Various birds

Plate 37 from *Ornithologiae Libri Tres . . .*, by Francis Willughby,
London, 1676

The part played by John Ray and Francis Willughby in systematically
classifying the plants and animals known to Europeans by the middle of
the seventeenth century has already been discussed (p. 20). Their work
was much in advance of the encyclopedists such as Gesner and Aldrovandi
and they set a pattern for systematic work which was to be implemented
less than a century later by Linnaeus who established the basic principles
of classification which are still used by scientists today. The text of the
above work on ornithology was prepared by Willughby; after his death
Ray edited it and saw it through the press. The illustrations are not of
outstanding quality but they are accurate and often charming; all
fabulous or doubtful birds were rigorously discarded. The birds
represented here are: Song Thrush *(Turdus ericetorum)*, Fieldfare
(Turdus pilaris), Blackbird *(Turdus merula)*, Blue Rock Thrush
(Monticola solitarius), Ring Ouzel *(Turdus torquatus)*, and Starling
(Sturnus vulgaris).

Engraving, 12 × 7·25 in. (305 × 184 mm.)

TAB. XXXVII.

Turdus simpliciter dictus. The Mavis or Song Thrush.

Turdus pilaris. The Fieldfare.

Merula. The Blackbird.

Passer solitarius mas Aldrov.

Sturnus. The Stare or Starling.

Merula torquata. The Ring Ouzell.

Sidney Parkinson

63

Fox Sparrow *(Passerella iliaca)*

Plate 14 from a volume of drawings by Sydney Parkinson, 1766–7,
British Museum

Sydney Parkinson (1745–71) was the young Scottish artist who won
undying fame for himself as the chief natural history painter in the
Endeavour, on Captain Cook's first voyage round the world (1768–71).
He served his apprenticeship for several years beforehand by working for
Thomas Pennant and Joseph Banks to whom he was introduced by James
Lee of the Vineyard Nursery at Hammersmith.

Parkinson was born in Edinburgh and was first apprenticed to a woollen
draper but his talent for drawing plants and animals attracted so much
favourable notice that, when he was about twenty, he and his widowed
mother moved to London where he immediately began exhibiting his
work with the Free Society. It seems probable that Lee, who came from
Selkirk near Edinburgh, knew the Parkinsons before they came south. At
all events the young man was engaged to teach Lee's talented daughter
Ann, then thirteen years old. She became one of the best natural history
painters of the period but almost none of her work was published.

Parkinson painted birds, fishes and insects collected by Banks in
Newfoundland and Labrador, and various exotic insects and birds that
Banks had acquired through his collectors. His chief work in the
Endeavour was to record the plants while they were fresh, and various
animals whenever there was time.

Little of Parkinson's work on Banks's Newfoundland collections was
published in the eighteenth century except for some engravings in some
editions of Pennant's *British Zoology*, where there is a handsome
engraving of eider ducks based on his painting of the Northern Common
Eider, and also in *Arctic Zoology* (1784–7) which contains a plate based
on his drawing of the Eskimo Curlew (see Plate 90).

Banks collected the Fox Sparrow in October 1766, at Croque, a port
on the east coast of the northern peninsula of Newfoundland where he
reported it as being fairly common in the open woodlands.

Watercolour, 9·85 × 8·3 in. (250 × 210 mm.)

64

Eagle Owl *(Bubo bubo)*, Long-eared Owl *(Asio otus)*, Short-eared Owl *(Asio flammeus)*

Plate 12 from *Ornithologiae Libri Tres . . .*, by Francis Willughby, London, 1676

The plates in this publication were collected from various sources; this engraving by F. H. van Houe (1628–98) is one of the best and most vigorous. This Dutch artist, who was born at The Hague but moved to London, has succeeded in portraying the owls with a degree of vitality that is remarkable when they are compared with the series of these birds engraved by Matthäus Merian for Joannes Jonston only twenty-five years earlier (see Plates 53 and 54). For other notes on Willughby see Plate 62.

Engraving, 12 × 7·25 in. (305 × 184 mm.)

TAB. XII.

Bubo.
The Great Eagle
Owle.

Otus sive Asio.
The Horn-Owle.

Scops Aldrov.
The Little Horn Owle.

F. H. Van Hove, Sculp.

No. 14.

Ein Breit Schnabelein.

No. 15.

Ein See Teuchel

No. 53.

Ein Graue Passer stelt.

No. 54.

Ein Gele Passer stelt.

65, 66

Shoveler *(Spatula clypeata)* and Great Crested Grebe *(Podiceps cristatus)*

Pied Wagtail *(Motacilla alba)* and Yellow Wagtail *(Motacilla flava)*

Folios 12 and 33 from *An Exact natural Description . . .*, by Leonhard Baldner, Strasbourg, 1653, manuscript, British Museum

Ray and Willughby met Baldner when they travelled through Europe in 1663–6, and Willughby then bought the volume of paintings and descriptions which is now in the British Museum, together with a volume of translation they commissioned of all Baldner's notes. The paintings are exquisitely detailed with decorations in black ink and gold leaf, so that they have some of the quality of the finest illuminated manuscripts of an earlier date. There are thirty-one pages of drawings of birds, usually two to a page; the rest of the volume consists of illustrations of fishes, crayfish, frogs and various invertebrates.

The foreword by Baldner begins thus:

At the first I had no design to write a Book of Fishes and Fowls, much less of Insects, but because I shot in the year 1645 some wonderfull Water-Fowls and made them to bee drawn to life, and as soon as I got the same, my Delight & Meditations I had of them prevailed with me to goe on. Thus in the name of the Lord I have let downe my Net and Fishers-yarne, and what I learnt thereby by thirty years Practice, delivered a little in writing in the year 1653, ye 31 of December.

Baldner's notes on the Great Crested Crebe give some idea of the kind of observations he made:

[It] is a very ravenous Fowl of Fishes, upon which he feedeth. Yea Hee eateth his own Feathers, for his Stomach is always full of them. This Fowl I shot, and some more I got which were taken in a Net. There are but few of them . . . Those of the Male Kind have a thick Crest of Feathers about the Head, being angry hee sets them up like as two Ears of an Ass . . . In posture he goes upright like a Man, but falls quickly again upon its Belly, for his Feet are more fit for swimming than for going . . .

Watercolour, ink and gold leaf on cartridge paper, each approximately 6 × 7·5 in. (152 × 190 mm.)

67

Golden Oriole *(Oriolus oriolus)*

Plate 11 from *Nederlandsche Vogelen . . .*, by Cornelis Nozeman, Vol. 1,
Amsterdam, 1770

Nozeman was a clergyman who was passionately interested in birds and
set to work to describe all the species that occurred in Holland; it was the
first time that such a comprehensive publication had been undertaken
in that country and he, like the earlier scholar Aldrovandi, did not live
long enough to see his life's task completed.

The Golden Oriole breeds in many parts of Europe and Asia. Other
species are also found in Asia and Africa.

Engraving, 16·5 × 10·7 in. (423 × 270 mm.)

68
OVERLEAF

A Seventeenth-Century Museum

Frontispiece to *Museum Wormianum, seu Historia rerum rariorum . . .*,
by Ole Worm, Leyden, 1655

Museums, as we now know them, date from the end of the fifteenth
century but they were then mostly collections of natural history and
archaeological material which seldom included birds; these were difficult
to preserve owing to the fact that they were only disembowelled and dried
so that within a few years beetles and other insects attacked the muscle
layer and the remains disintegrated. The Egyptians preserved the ibis,
which was sacred to them, by mummifying the corpses just as they
would those of human beings. It was not until the end of the eighteenth
century that the skinning of birds in preparing museum material came
into practice. Ole Worm's museum was one of the few early ones in which
birds were shown. See also Plate 96.

Engraving, 10·85 × 14·05 in. (275 × 358 mm.)

69, 70, 71, 72
OVERLEAF

Nightingales being encouraged to sing, then being prepared for a pie: Immature Lesser or Great Grey Shrike *(Lanius minor* or *L. excubitor)*: Cuckoo *(Cuculus canorus)*

Plates facing pages 3, 5, 38 and 41 from *Uccelliera overo discorso della
natura . . .*, by G. P. Olina, Rome, 1684 (first edition 1622)

Olina's book was the first ornithological text in which engravings were
used as illustrations *per se*, and not merely as an adjunct to the letterpress.
The plates showing nightingales being encouraged to sing by a concourse
of players (Plate 69), and then being prepared for a pie (Plate 70),
necessitating the slaughter of large numbers, typify the ambivalence
shown by many people, both then and now, to birds and other animals.
The engraving of the shrike with its prey (Plate 71) is a good early
example of the better kind of natural history illustration.

Engravings, each 8·75 × 6·1 in. (223 × 155 mm.)

ORIOLUS.

Orioli e Nitidiſſima Collectione Dominorum RENSSELAAR, Ams...
Nidus vero ſuppeditatus a Reverendo Viro A: BVVRT, V.D.M. Amst...

MUSEI
WORMIANI
HISTORIA
LUGD · BATAVORUM
EX OFFICINA ELSEVIRIANA

Caftrica·Palombina·

Cuculo.

BIRD and FLOWER of PORT JACKSON *Natural Size* 1789

73

Kookaburra *(Dacelo gigas)*

Folio 57 from a collection of drawings by George Raper, *c.*1788,
British Museum (Natural History)

This Australian bird is one of the largest members of the kingfisher
family, the Alcedinae, which is found in most parts of the world save for
the polar regions and other high latitudes. In spite of their popular name
many kingfishers do not live mainly on fish but take insects on land; one
unusual species has a flattened bill with which it has been seen digging
for earthworms.

Kookaburras, also known as Laughing Jackasses, are usually found in
pairs or small parties. They have an extraordinary laughing call,
frequently heard in parks and gardens. They eat small reptiles as well as
insects, and sometimes rob the nests of other birds. Originally confined
to eastern and southern Australia, they have now spread to other areas and
to Tasmania.

George Raper was a midshipman in H.M.S. *Sirius*, a ship of the First
Fleet, which sailed to Australia in 1787. His painting of the Kookaburra
was not the first, since an illustration had already been published of one
of these birds collected by Joseph Banks on the eastern coast of Australia
during the voyage of the *Endeavour*. When Captain Cook finally reached
the Cape of Good Hope, after the terrible epidemic that had swept so
disastrously through the ship, Banks met a young French naturalist there
who was on his way to work with Philibert Commerson (a doctor and
biologist who had sailed with Bougainville round the world as far as
Mauritius, where he remained to make further collections). Banks gave
the young Frenchman, Pierre Sonnerat, some of his Australian birds. An
engraving of a Kookaburra, almost certainly made from one of Banks's
specimens, appeared with plates of various South American birds (Plate
95) which Sonnerat abstracted from Commerson's collections after his
death in 1773. These were all published in a volume entitled *Voyage à la
Nouvelle Guinée* (1776), a country in which Sonnerat had never set foot,
and where the Kookaburra does not occur.

Most of the land birds collected by Banks and Solander in Australia
and New Zealand seem to have disappeared during the latter part of the
voyage, probably because Banks had by then lost most of the members of
his staff and was unable to care adequately for his collection of skins.
Sonnerat's plate is therefore of considerable historical interest but as an
engraving it is rather dull. Raper's watercolour is a much more
sympathetic study of this handsome bird.

Watercolour, 19·3 × 12·7 in. (494 × 322 mm.)

74
Various birds

Folio 391 from *The Memoirs of Babur*, with illustrations by Ustad Mansur, undated, Department of Oriental Manuscripts, British Museum

The splendid illuminations in this Mogul manuscript are by Mansur, who began work in the reign of Akbar and achieved such mastery of his medium in the reign (1605–27) of Jehangir that the emperor gave him the titles of Nadir-Al-Asr, Master of the Age, and Ustad, Master; it is the second appellation that has remained so that he is widely known today as Ustad Mansur. Jehangir actually wrote on one of the bird paintings in which Mansur specialized: 'This is a picture of a bird called jurz i barr painted by Ustad Mansur, the most eminent painter of his time. Written by Jehangir Akbar, Shah, in the year 19 [AD 1624] of his reign.'

The Mogul artists began to develop an interest in ornithology under Akbar, and this developed until in the seventeenth century they were among the finest bird painters of all time. A number of Mansur's signed paintings have survived and are to be seen in western collections as well as in Indian ones.

The page selected from Babur's memoirs shows the painter's decorative skill, and a variety of birds with which he was familiar. Babur himself lived long before (1483–1530). The first of the Mogul emperors, he was a fascinating character; a brave and dashing soldier, he was also an able administrator, a keen gardener—one of the folios in this volume shows him inspecting the work of some gardeners—and a gifted writer. His autobiography has been translated into English many times.

Watercolour on vellum, 11·6 × 6·5 in. (295 × 165 mm.)

پشت مرد و بال او سفید است و آواز بلند یی دارد و رنگ

دیگر پرندهٔ اول و چشم سیاه یک برک سفید یت مانن ولاینها میرود از

از برک خیلی بلند تر است و از برک مند و بستان خورد تر است

یک مرغابی دیگر است و غز مپای میگویند از سو به پور چین کلاسر است

عمل سنکر کراتی

C. *Het Konings Vogeltje.*   D. *De Ambonsche Lang-bek.*

P. Goeree delin. et fc. direxit.

75

King Bird of Paradise *(Cicinnurus regius)*
?Whimbrel *(Numenius phaeopus)*

Plate facing page 312 from *Omstandig Verhaal van de Geschiedenissen . . . in Ambonia*, by François Valentijn, Amsterdam, 1724–6

François Valentijn (1666–1727), a priest, was sent from Holland to the East Indies in 1685. In Amboina he met the gifted naturalist Rumphius, who seems to have inspired him to keep detailed observations, so that the ample collections of specimens he obtained during his various journeys in the East Indies were well documented. He returned to Holland in 1695 and remained there for ten years before sailing again to the East. He finally returned to Holland in 1714 and wrote up his material. Among other important finds was the King Bird of Paradise, beautifully described by A. R. Wallace (Plate 130) a century and a half later:

> It was a small bird, a little less than a thrush. The greater part of its plumage was of an intense cinnabar red, with a gloss as of spun glass. On the head the feathers became short and velvety and shaded into rich orange. Beneath, from the breast downwards, was pure white, with the softness and gloss of silk, and across the breast a band of deep metallic green separated this colour from the red of the throat . . . Merely in arrangement of colours and texture of plumage this little bird was a gem of the first water.

Valentijn also collected the Black Sickle-billed Bird of Paradise (Plate 139). In spite of the relative sobriety of its plumage this was a popular article of trade, as Valentijn remarked.

Engraving, 10·75 × 6·9 in. (273 × 175 mm.)

76

Blue-faced Honey Eater *(Entomyza cyanotis)*

Folio 48 from a collection of drawings by George Raper, *c.*1788,
British Museum (Natural History)

The Blue-faced Honey Eater is a bird of the open country in eastern
Australia, ranging from northern Queensland to South Australia.
Members of this species are usually seen in pairs or small flocks. They are
especially abundant in the vicinity of Pandanus Palms in Queensland, and
are often called Pandanus Birds on that account.

The blue flower in this painting is the Australian Wild Iris which,
although a member of the Iridaceae, does not belong to the genus
Iris but to *Patersonia*; the small pink flower is a species of *Drosera*.

George Raper was born about 1768; although the date of his death is
usually given as 1797 there is evidence that he lived until the end of 1798
or a little later. His mother was given letters of administration over his
estate in March 1799. He entered the navy in 1783, joined H.M.S.
Sirius as an A.B. in 1787 and sailed with the First Fleet to Australia that
year. There was no official artist in the fleet but several officers in the
Sirius had considerable artistic ability. The normal training of naval
officers included drawing as an aid to their cartographical work, and it is
probable that Raper developed his natural ability through watching some
of the others at work. He was promoted to the rank of midshipman
during the voyage.

There are three sets of Raper drawings in public collections: the first
and largest is in the British Museum (Natural History), from which this
example and Plate 73 are taken. The set consists of seventy-three sheets,
all but seven of which are signed by Raper. A second set is in the
Mitchell Library, Sydney and a third in the Alexander Turnbull Library,
Wellington, New Zealand. Not all the work in these two collections is by
Raper and some of the paintings are copies.

Watercolour, 18·55 × 13·2 in. (470 × 332 mm.)

BIRD & FLOWER of PORT JACKSON *Natural Size* —

The Manofwar-bird, and the Chinees Fish, &c all etched on the copper plate from life by George Edwards, July the first, A 1758.

309

77
Greater Frigate-Bird, Hen *(Fregata minor)*

Plate 309 from *Gleanings of Natural History*, by George Edwards, Vols.
5–7, London, 1758

George Edwards (1694–1773) is often considered to be the father of
British ornithology, although his work included descriptions and
illustrations of many exotic species as well as natives of Britain. He was
naturally gifted as a scientist and a draughtsman, and he was also
fortunate in attracting the friendship of men such as Sir Hans Sloane
and Mark Catesby (Plates 41, 45). For many years he made drawings of
animals for Sloane, and when he began to consider writing and illustrating
his own book of birds, Catesby taught him the technique of engraving,
as he himself says in his introduction to *Gleanings of Natural History*:

> I was discouraged, upon first thinking of this work, at the great expense of
> graving, printing, and other things, which I knew would be a certain cost
> attended with a very uncertain profit, till my good friend Mr. Catesby
> put me on etching my plates myself, as he had done in all his work: and
> not only so, but invited me to see him at work at etching, and gave me
> all the hints and instructions to proceed, which favour I think myself
> obliged publicly to acknowledge.

Sloane was instrumental in Edwards being appointed librarian of the
Royal College of Physicians, which gave him both a salary and time to
continue with his writing and editing. He borrowed specimens or visited
many houses where tropical and other birds were kept as pets in order
to extend the range of his writings. His books are interesting, and amongst
other things they show how widespread the interest in natural history was
in England during the first half of the eighteenth century.

Frigate-birds may be seen in most tropical and subtropical seas,
particularly where there are abundant flying fish since they catch most
of their prey on the wing. They also pursue other birds and make them
disgorge their food. Their oil glands are small so that they are liable to
become waterlogged if they remain in the water for long. For this
reason they do not wander very far from land, and so have always been
regarded by mariners as a sign that they were approaching a coast. They
are magnificent birds in the air, a fitting portent of good fortune.

Etching 9·1 × 7·2 in. (232 × 178 mm.)

78

Eastern Turtle Dove *(Streptopelia orientalis)* with some characteristics of the Spotted Dove *(S. chinensis)*

Plate 31 from the collection of John Reeves (1774–1856), British Museum (Natural History)

This dove seems to have been painted from birds belonging to two species but has its own charm, and is representative of much Chinese bird painting of the eighteenth century, long after the ideals of accurate representation instilled by Hui-tsung (Plate 6) had lapsed.

John Reeves, a Fellow of the Royal Society, was active in sending plants and drawings to his friends and family in England, and the British Museum (Natural History) has a most interesting collection of paintings of plants and animals by Chinese artists which he accumulated while he was living in Canton, where he was an Inspector of Tea.

Watercolour, 13·4 × 12·25 in. (340 × 311 mm.)

班鳩

Dessiné et Gravé par Martinet

1. Gobe-Mouche huppé, du Cap de Bonne-Espérance.
2. Gobe-Mouche blanc huppé, du Cap de Bonne-Espérance.

f. m. Martinet.

Jacana, du Mexique.

79, 80

Paradise Flycatchers *(Terpsiphone* spp.*)*
Jacana *(Jacana ?spinosa)*

Plate 234 from Vol. 5 and Plate 322 from Vol. 9 of *Histoire Naturelle des Oiseaux*, by G. L. L. de Buffon, Paris, 1781–6

Georges Louis Leclerc, Compte de Buffon (1707–88) made notable contributions to zoology in the eighteenth century. He was one of the first to recognize that all living organisms were fundamentally similar, whether they were plant or animal, and that life itself was a physical characteristic of matter and not a metaphysical property.

He was also one of the earliest writers to plan a true natural history, embracing the whole biological kingdom; this resulted in a work of forty-four volumes, *Histoire Naturelle,–avec la description du Cabinet du Roi*, which was not completed until 1804, long after his death.

Paradise Flycatchers are found in Africa and across Asia to Japan. The males are distinguished by their long tails, and by the assumption of a largely white plumage for at least some part of the year, while the females are generally glossy chestnut, though in both sexes the crown is a shining steel-blue.

Jacanas belong to the Charadriiformes but their precise relationships are obscure. All of them have enormously elongated toes and claws that enable them to run lightly over the floating leaves of water lilies and other aquatic plants. The eggs are shiny from a cuticular form of waterproofing which is useful since they are often at least partially submerged. Some species appear to be able to hold the eggs and young against the body, in a kind of pocket formed by the wing. Jacana is a Brazilian word but it has become the name for all the known species. They are found not only in South and Central America, but also in Africa, Asia and Australia, ranging from sea-level to 8,000 feet. For the most part they live in the sheltered shallows of inland waters.

Engravings, 8·5 × 7·25 (216 × 184 mm.) and 8·9 × 7·25 (224 × 174 mm.)

81, 82

Canada Goose *(Branta canadensis)*
Common Guillemot *(Uria aalge)* and Puffin
(Fratercula arctica)

Plates 26 and 6 from Vol. 6 of *Ornithologie . . .*, by M. J. Brisson,
Paris, 1760

Mathurin Jacques Brisson (1723–1806) made a special study of birds in
his youth. He had a very precise and orderly mind and was well versed in
the literature of ornithology. Beginning as a pupil of Réaumur, an
exceedingly able entomologist and physicist, Brisson later became his
collaborator and looked after his very valuable collection of birds, many
of which were exotic species collected by Pierre Poivre in Mauritius and
Cochin-China. (Poivre rose to fame by breaking the Dutch monopoly of
the spice trade, illegally and successfully introducing nutmegs from the
Moluccas into Mauritius.)

Brisson set to work to classify birds more carefully and systematically
than anyone had done since Willughby (Plates 62, 64), and, although his
system was not binomial, it was in many ways an advance on that of
Linnaeus. He dealt with 1,336 species. His book was illustrated by
Martinet, who was trained as an engineer but eventually worked as a
draughtsman and engraver. After the death in 1757 of Réaumur, Brisson
in his turn became a physicist.

Canada Geese breed in Alaska, Canada and the northern part of the
United States; they were introduced into Great Britain in the seventeenth
century and breed there also. For other guillemots and puffins see Plates
141 and 105.

Engravings, 8·2 × 10·5 in. (210 × 267 mm.) and 7 × 8·5 in. (178 × 216 mm.)

Echelle de 6. pouces.

Dessiné et Gravé par Martinet.

1. *Guillemot*.   2. *Macareux*.

83

Port Lincoln Parrot *(Platycercus zonarius)*

Plate 20 from the zoological drawings of F. L. Bauer, British Museum
(Natural History)

One of the most gifted European artists to come to England in the latter
part of the eighteenth century, Ferdinand Lucas Bauer (1760–1826) is
nevertheless less well known than his equally able brother Francis,
celebrated for his botanical paintings most of which were executed at
the Royal Botanic Gardens, Kew, where he worked for fifty years. F. L.
Bauer was more adventurous than his older brother and as a young man
travelled to Greece with Sibthorp, in order to illustrate his work on the
Greek flora. Later he travelled to Australia with Matthew Flinders and
Robert Brown. He painted not only the Australian plants but a number of
birds and other animals. He used watercolour but he also worked in oils.
Some very fine still-life paintings with birds and fruit have survived.

This painting of an Australian parrot seems to represent *Platycercus
zonarius* more closely than a form which it intergrades, known popularly
as Twenty-Eight from its curious call.

Watercolour, 19·75 × 13 in. (502 × 330 mm.)

84

Cockatiel or Quarrion *(Nymphicus hollandicus)*

Plate 27 from *Illustrations of the Family of Psittacidae . . . drawn from life and on stone,* by Edward Lear, London, 1832

One of the most accomplished of all bird painters, Edward Lear (1812–88) was, apart from some elementary tuition from one of his sisters, entirely self-trained as a draughtsman, painter and lithographer. He began to earn money with his drawings at the age of fifteen, and was later employed by Gould, although his name does not always appear in the books in which he participated. His lithographic studies of birds, particularly those of parrots, are very fine indeed. Whether he knew of the ornithological lithographs by Webb-Smith and D'Oyly (Plate 126), which appeared two or three years before his own, is uncertain.

Lithograph, 19·5 × 13 in. (495 × 330 mm.)

85

OVERLEAF

Domestic Pigeon, Feather-footed ('muffed') variety *(Columba livia)*

Plate 283 from *Ornithologia Methodice Digesta . . . Illuminatis Ornata,* by Xaverio Manetti, Vol. 3, Florence, 1767–76

Xaverio Manetti (1723–84) was the author of one of the most sumptuous, illustrated bird books of the eighteenth century although he made no special contribution to the scientific development of ornithology. His text was both in Latin and Italian, and the five volumes contain altogether six hundred hand-coloured engravings of all sorts of birds, domestic varieties, as well as those wild ones that could be seen in Italy.

The plates have remarkable vitality and the pigeon shown in this plate possesses a comfortable appearance of self-assurance that offers a curious contrast to the equally self-assured plucked fowl, engraved by Stubbs (opposite), which seems to be just as full of life. See also Plate 30.

Engraving and watercolour, 13·2 × 10·1 in. (340 × 272 mm.)

86

OVERLEAF

A plucked fowl

Plate 10 from *Comparative Anatomy,* by George Stubbs, London, 1804–6

George Stubbs (1724–1806) studied anatomy at York, but his great knowledge of the structure of the horse was gained by the laborious dissection, muscle layer by muscle layer, of a corpse, suspended by chains and slowly stripped down to the skeleton. When he was thirty years old he visited Morocco and Italy, and thereafter gradually acquired fame as an animal painter.

This plate of a fowl is taken from a volume of the plates used to illustrate his book *A Comparative Anatomical exposition of the structure of the Human Body with that of a Tiger and Common Fowl.*

Engraving, 19 × 14·75 in. (482 × 379 mm.)

PALÆORNIS NOVÆ-HOLLANDIÆ.

New Holland Parrakeet,

in the Possession of the Right Hon. the Countess of Mountcharles.

1 Male 2 Female.

E. Lear, del. et lith. 29   Printed by C. Hullmandel.

Colombo d. Piccion grosso Reale con penne ai piedi. Columba domestica maior pedibus pennatis, sive Dasypes.

TAB. X.

VULTUR GRYPHUS Lin.

A. Humboldt del.ᵗ Barraband perf.ᵗ   Bouquet sculp.ᵗ l.aɴ

87

Condor *(Vultur gryphus)*

Plate 8 from *Recueil d'Observations de Zoologie et d'anatomie comparée . . .*,
by Al. de Humboldt and A. Bonpland, Vol. 1, Paris, 1811

It is fitting that Humboldt, one of the greatest of all the explorers of
South America, should be represented here by his plate of the Condor,
one of the largest of all volant birds, with a wing span of nine feet nine
inches. (Wandering Albatrosses, however, may exceed this by two feet.)
The size and ferocity of the Condor were so much exaggerated by early
travellers that Ray regarded it as a largely mythical species and refused to
include it in Willughby's *Ornithology* (Plates 62, 64).

Humboldt (1769–1859) was educated at Göttingen, then proceeded to
the mining school at Freiburg as a pupil of Werner. He worked in mines
for several years and thus became familiar with the use of various kinds of
physical apparatus; it was only later that he turned his attention to botany
and zoology. When a young man he travelled on the Rhine with George
Forster, assistant naturalist on Captain Cook's second voyage round the
world. Forster's account of tropical life fired Humboldt with the desire to
travel in equatorial regions and he planned to visit Africa. Since this was
prevented by political troubles, he decided instead to explore the Spanish
dominions in South America. After a somewhat hazardous journey he
reached the Caribbean, and with his friend Bonpland spent the next five
years first in the region of the Orinoco, then in western South America.
His *Personal Narrative* is one of the most readable of all travel books
although it covers only the first part of his journey. Travellers sailing from
the Panama Canal across the Pacific are sharply aware of the cold current
that bears his name, since it sweeps up from the Antarctic past the
Galapagos Islands, and enables penguins to breed there, in a much lower
latitude than elsewhere.

Engraving, 11·2 × 9·5 in. (333 × 240 mm.)

88

Turkey *(Meleagris gallopavo)*

Plate 67 from *Illustrations of the American Ornithology of Alexander Wilson and Charles Lucian Bonaparte . . .*, by Captain Thomas Brown, Edinburgh, 1831

Alexander Wilson (1766–1813) gave great impetus to the study of American birds. Born in Scotland, he sailed to America in 1794. He was a profoundly able naturalist, his great ambition was to study and describe as many species as he could, and to write a competent *American Ornithology*. Lack of financial backing, poor health and his early death at the age of forty-seven, prevented the fulfilment of his hopes, but he rather than Audubon is regarded by a very large number of professional ornithologists as the founder of American ornithology in its present form. Audubon was nevertheless a more competent painter and was able to design on a large scale. He was also extremely ambitious and wrote to one of his friends, when he found that Wilson's work was being prepared for publication: 'I will push my publication with such unremitting vigour that my book will come before the public before Wilson's can be got out.' He succeeded and both Wilson's own work and the above compilation by Brown (from various sources) were not able to compete when it came to sales.

Some of Brown's plates are very fine; others, such as one showing a Snowy Owl sitting on a southern magnolia tree, are unfortunate. This illustration of the turkeys is one of the most attractive. The bibliographic history of Brown's publication is interesting. It has been discussed by W. Faxon in two numbers of *The Auk* (1903 : 236–41 ; 1919 : 623–6).

Engraving, 19 × 14·1 in. (482 × 358 mm.)

WILD TURKEY. *Meleagris Gallopavo* 1 Male. 2 Female. 3 Young

P. Mazell sculp.

Passenger Pigeon. N.º 187.　　*Carolina Pigeon. N.º 186.*

P. Mazell sculp.

Eskimaux Curlew. N.º 364.　　*Little Woodcock. N.*

89, 90

Passenger Pigeons *(Ectopistes migratorius)*

Eskimo Curlew *(Numenius borealis)* and American Woodcock *(Philohela minor)*

Plates 14 and 19 from *Arctic Zoology*, Vol. 2, by Thomas Pennant, London, 1787

The engraving of the Passenger Pigeons shows a male above, and below it a female which Pennant thought was another species. The enormous abundance of these birds was noted by the early explorers in the seventeenth century. Pennant (p. 324) remarks that Josselyn 'who observed these pigeons in 1638, in *New England* before they were disturbed by population, says he has seen flights of them moving at *Michaelmas* to the southward four or five miles long, so thick that he lost sight of the sun'. This was confirmed by Alexander Wilson (Plate 88) nearly two centuries later:

> Happening to go ashore, one charming afternoon, to purchase some milk . . . while talking with the people within doors, I was suddenly struck with astonishment at a loud rushing roar, succeeded by an instant darkening which, on the first moment, I took for a tornado, about to overwhelm the house . . . The people . . . coolly said "It is only the Pigeons". When they have frequented one of these places for some time [for nesting], the appearance it exhibits is surprising. The ground is covered to the depth of several inches with their dung; all the tender grass and underwood is destroyed; the surface strewn with large limbs of trees, broken down by the weight of the birds clustering one above another; and the trees themselves for thousands of acres, killed as completely as if girdled with an axe. The marks of this desolation remain for many years.

These pigeons were utilized as food on an enormous scale; they are now extinct. A similar fate has almost overtaken the Eskimo Curlew, an Arctic breeding species which in the autumn migrated south to eastern Argentina. It too was present in large numbers though not as abundant as the pigeons. For a long time it was thought to be extinct but a few pairs have been reported in recent years.

Pennant's book on the zoology of the Arctic was one of the first on zoogeography to appear. He had a very good mind, with a wide variety of interests, natural history and antiquities being predominant amongst them. He will always be remembered by English people for having been one of the two correspondents to whom Gilbert White wrote from Selborne. See also Plate 139 and p. 21.

Engravings, 6·7 × 5·5 in. (170 × 140 mm.) and 6·7 × 5·65 in. (170 × 145 mm.)

91, 92

Bearded Penguin *(Pygoscelis antarctica)*
Antarctic Petrel *(Thalassoica antarctica)*

Plates 82 and 95 from Vol. 1 of original drawings by Georg Forster, 1772–5, British Museum (Natural History)

Both these drawings were made by Georg Forster (1754–94) during the winter of 1772–3 on Captain Cook's second voyage round the world. The scientific observations made on oceanic birds during Cook's voyages were the earliest documented records of these groups of species, and are extremely valuable on that account. From the first voyage Banks and Solander brought back detailed descriptions of albatrosses and petrels; the Forsters added to these and published drawings and descriptions of much of the material including four species of penguins, amongst them the Bearded Penguin figured here. The wash drawing of the Antarctic Petrel is one of earliest depicting any petrel in flight. There is another version of it made after the return of the *Resolution* to England when Georg Forster and his father J. R. Forster expected to be presented to George III. With this in mind they selected thirty of the most interesting paintings and had them copied by a professional artist, intending them as a gift to the king. Owing to the fact that J. R. Forster quarrelled with Cook and the Admiralty over the writing of the official account of the voyage, they failed to meet the king and make the presentation. Georg Forster took the copies of the paintings abroad – the originals were purchased by Joseph Banks – and sold them. They were lost to sight for nearly two centuries but rediscovered after the Second World War in a library at Gotha, East Germany. They have now all been handsomely published. The rather brightly coloured copy in the Gotha set lacks much of the feeling possessed by this sombre version. Antarctic Petrels occur only in high latitudes and the amount of ice round the *Resolution* made it difficult for the Forsters to collect the birds they were able to shoot from the ship.

Watercolours, 19·5 × 13·7 in. (495 × 348 mm.) and 14·2 × 21 in. (359 × 533 mm.)

PLATE. CII.

Blue Jay,

CORVUS CRISTATUS,

Male. 1. Female. 2.3.

Drawn from nature by J.J. Audubon F.R.S. F.L.S.

Engraved, printed & Coloured by R. Havell.

93

Blue Jay *(Cyanocitta cristata)*

Plate 102 from *The Birds of America,* by J. J. Audubon, Vol. 2, London,
1831–4

This is a typical piece of design by J. J. Audubon (1785–1851), somewhat
flamboyant and with no great appreciation of the anatomy of the living
bird. The story of his life is too well known to need repetition here.
Let is be said that his work was one of the great money-spinners of
ornithological texts even in the nineteenth century; his paintings still
fetch enormous prices. He has always aroused as much criticism as
enthusiasm; sometimes he has been credited with all sorts of innovations
in the history of bird illustration, such as the representation of birds with
their prey or food plants. That this is unjustified will be apparent to
anyone who looks through the plates in this volume, beginning with the
figure of a gull swallowing a fish which is believed to be a copy of a
painting of the third century BC. Reproductions of Audubon's paintings
have given pleasure to many thousands of people. See also Plate 88.

Engraving, 26·25 × 21 in. (667 × 533 mm.)

94

Chimborazian Hill-Star *(Oreotrochilus chimborazo)*

Plate 68 from *A Monograph of the Trochilidae* . . ., by John Gould,
Vol. 2, London, 1861

Humming-birds are sometimes believed to be confined to subtropical and
tropical climates where they live exclusively on nectar obtained from
flowers. In fact they are widely distributed from sea-level to the upper
limits of flowering plants on the mountains of North and South America,
and insects form an appreciable part of their food. Some species have
toothed bills to facilitate the capture of their prey.

Gould made a large collection of these birds and his monograph of
the family consists of five volumes. *Oreotrochilus chimborazo* is confined
to the slopes of Mount Chimborazo at altitudes of twelve to sixteen
thousand feet. It lives on the honey of, and the insects attracted to, the
shrub *Chuquiraga insignis* shown in this plate. Mount Chimborazo can
be seen faintly in the background.

The early explorers of the Americas were as fascinated by humming-
birds as we are today. In Samuel Purchas's *Purchas his Pilgrimes* (1625)
he wrote:

> In Peru there are birds which they call *Tomineios*, so small that
> often-times I have doubted seeing them flie whether they were Bees or
> Butter-flies; but in truth they are birds. . . . In *New Spain* there are
> abundance of [humming-] birds with excellent feathers, so as there bee
> not any found in *Europe* that comes near them, as we may see by the
> Images of feathers they bring from thence, the which are (with great
> reason) much valued and esteemed . . . as they seeme properly to be the
> true colours of a Painter, and have so lively and pleasing a regard as the
> Painter cannot exceed it with his pencill and colours. . . . It is a goodly
> thing to see the lustre, which a greene, an orange tawnie like gold, and
> other fine colours do cast, and beholding them another way they seeme
> dead colours.

The use of real feathers in portraying birds against a painted background
was practised off and on until the eighteenth century. Early British
exhibition catalogues note the use of such a technique; Peter Paillou
(Plate 101) was amongst the artists who practised it, though he used a
more conventional technique in the plate reproduced in this volume.

Lithograph, 20 × 14 in. (508 × 356 mm.)

OREOTROCHILUS CHIMBORAZO.

P. Sonnerat Pinx.   C. Baquoy Sculp

Le Manchot de la Nouvelle Guinée.

95

King Penguin *(Aptenodytes patagonica)*

Plate 113 from *Voyage à la Nouvelle Guiné*e, by P. Sonnerat, Paris, 1776

Although this engraving is signed by Sonnerat, the original was not his work but a drawing by Jossigny, the draughtsman who sailed with Commerson, the naturalist on Bougainville's voyage round the world (1766–9). King Penguins live in the Antarctic and sub-Antarctic seas, breeding on the islands there. Commerson made extensive collections of plants and animals in and about Tierra del Fuego, and kept his material with him when Bougainville left him at Mauritius on the return voyage. Poivre, the Intendant of Mauritius, and Commerson planned to make a biological survey of the island; Sonnerat was sent from France to act as assistant to Commerson, who died from overwork. Sonnerat then came into possession of his material. Ambitious and unscrupulous, he used Jossigny's drawings to illustrate a book about New Guinea although, as pointed out elsewhere (Plate 73), he had never been there. His misdeeds were known to Cuvier and others, then apparently forgotten, and for many years ornithologists speculated how penguins of the Antarctic could have been found in New Guinea. Poivre and Sonnerat were instrumental in breaking the Dutch spice monopoly (Plate 81) and this may have been the reason why Sonnerat, apparently, was not disgraced.

Engraving, 7·75 × 5·9 in. (197 × 149 mm.)

96

Great Auk *(Alca impennis)*

Plate facing page 300 from *Museum Wormianum, seu Historia rerum rariorum . . .*, by Ole Worm, Leyden, 1655

Ole Worm (1588–1654), a Danish archaeologist and physician, set up a museum in Copenhagen. His Great Auk was a pet rather than a specimen; the engraving shows the white collar which led imitators to draw these birds with a ring of white feathers round the neck. There are many kinds of auk; they are birds of the northern hemisphere, and are particularly abundant in the northern seas in the vicinity of the Arctic Circle. (They are unrelated to penguins which are confined to the southern hemisphere.)

Pennant wrote of the Great Auk in his *British Zoology* :

This bird is observed by seamen never to wander beyond soundings; and according to its appearance they direct their measures, being then assured that land is not very remote. Thus the modern sailors pay attention to auguries, in the same manner as *Aristophanes* tells us that those of *Greece* did above two thousand years ago.

From birds, in sailing men instructions take,
Now lye in port; now sail and profit make.

This was so true in the eighteenth century that various editions of the *English Pilot* figured Great Auks, which were very abundant, as indicators of the Newfoundland Banks; they are now extinct.

Engraving, 7·7 × 5·1 in. (195 × 130 mm.)

97
Storm-Petrel *(Hydrobates pelagica)*

Plate 126 from *Nederlandsche Vogelen . . .*, by Cornelis Nozeman, Vol. 3, Amsterdam, 1770–97

The petrels are essentially oceanic birds and never come to land save for breeding. They are then nocturnal, but at sea they are active during the day and this species characteristically follows vessels. It is widespread in the eastern north Atlantic and occurs also in the Mediterranean and off the south-west coast of Africa.

The Storm-Petrel is one of the small group of these birds commonly known as Mother Carey's Chickens, believed to be harbingers of bad weather at sea. For other work by Nozeman see Plate 67.

Engraving, 13·4 × 11 in. (342 × 279 mm.)

PHAROMACRUS MOCINNO.

J.Gould & W.Hart del. et lith.   Walter Imp.

98

Quetzal *(Pharomachrus mocino)*

Plate 1 from *A Monograph of the Trogonidae . . .*, by John Gould, London, 1875

The Quetzal is a trogon of the mountain forests from southern Mexico to the Panama region. One of the most splendid of all birds, it was sacred to the Mayas and Incas before the Spanish Conquest, and no one was allowed to kill it, although feathers might be taken for a special purpose. It is quite small, scarcely as large as a small domestic pigeon, but the male has long lustrous green tail feathers which make it appear larger than it actually is.

Hernández (p. 19) was the first European to describe the Quetzal; his account was carefully copied by Willughby (Plates 62, 64) but very little was known about this bird until the early nineteenth century. Cuvier was so astonished at the aspect of a specimen that he thought it an artificial production.

Lithograph, 20·5 × 13·75 in. (521 × 349 mm.)

99
Crested Cassicus *(Ostinops decumanus)*

Plate 44 from *Oiseaux brillans et remarquables du Brésil . . .*, by J. T. Descourtilz, 1835

It does not appear that this volume was published, technically speaking, since the text was handwritten although the plates, lithographed by Caltier, were printed. Descourtilz worked at the Museu Nacional in Rio de Janeiro. A first-class naturalist painter, he died young from poisoning while he was experimenting with a medicine for birds.

The bird figured here is common in many parts of Brazil and frequents gardens and orchards where its pleasant song is a familiar sound.

Lithograph, 16 × 11 in. (406 × 280 mm.)

100
OVERLEAF
Secretary-bird *(Sagittarius serpentarius)*

Plate XXVIII from *Cimelia Physica*, by George Shaw, London, 1796

An earlier edition of this book appeared as *Various subjects of Natural History, wherein are delineated Birds, Animals and many curious Plants etc.*, by J. F. Miller. It came out in parts from 1776 to 1785. Miller worked for Sir Joseph Banks and therefore had access to extensive collections of plants and animals. Shaw worked at the British Museum and supplied the text for Miller's plates.

Secretary-birds walk about with great elegance, spending most of their lives on the ground. They live on a wide variety of animals, including some other birds and insects. They are immensely valuable in that they prey largely on snakes which they kill by pounding them with their feet; they protect themselves against poisonous species by using their wings as shields against their bites.

Engraving, 17·6 × 10·75 in. (452 × 273 mm.)

Cassique Huppé

J. Theod. Descourtils del.

Lith. de Callier.

Falco serpentarius.

Tab. XXXIV.

The Cock of the Wood. Urogallus maior Mas. Der Auerhahn.

MERGANETTA FRENATA
♂ Central Chili (H.B.James) Type
♂ B.M.R. 92.2.10.330

101

ON PREVIOUS PAGE

Capercaillie *(Tetrao urogallus)*

Plate 34 from *Zoologica Britannica tabulis aeneis CXXXII illustrata,* by
T. Pennant, Augsburg, 1771

This painting of a Capercaillie is by Peter Paillou about whose life
little is known although he seems to have flourished from about 1740 to
1790. He executed many bird paintings for Pennant and Sir Joseph
Banks, and is best known for the illustrations to the *British Zoology*
(1766), in which all the plates are hand-coloured. The Augsburg edition
is a particularly impressive one from the point of view of the plates, but
it lacks the note on publication that appeared in the London edition:
'Published under the Inspection of the Cymmrodorion Society instituted
for the Promoting Useful Charities, and the Knowledge of Nature, among
the Descendants of the Ancient Britons. . . . Sold for the benefit of the
British Charity School. Clerkenwell Green.' Pennant was not only a
good zoologist, with a special interest in ornithology, he was also a
passionate geographer and antiquarian, with a great knowledge of his
own country. His preface to the first edition begins thus:

> At a time, when the study of natural history seems to revive in Europe;
> and the pens of several illustrious foreigners have been employed in
> enumerating the productions of their respective countries, we are
> unwilling that our own island should remain insensible to its particular
> advantages: . . . Do the heights of *Torburg,* or *Swucku* afford more
> instruction to the naturalist than the mountains of *Skiddaw* or *Snowdon?*
> whose sides are covered with a rich variety of uncommon vegetables
> while their bowels are replete with the most useful minerals . . .

Engraving, 18·5 × 11·6 in. (470 × 293 mm.)

102

Chilean Torrent Duck *(Merganetta armata)*

Folio 26 from Vol. 5 of *Anatidae,* by Henry Jones, unpublished, *c.* 1890,
Zoological Society, London

The Chilean Torrent Duck is one of the six forms of these somewhat
aberrant ducks that live besides the rushing streams and rivers of the
Andean chain and its foothills in western South America. For a note on
Jones see Plate 134.

Watercolour, 10·4 × 14·1 in. (264 × 366 mm.)

103

Narina Trogon *(Trogon narina)*

Plate 26 from *A Monograph of the Trogonidae . . .*, by John Gould,
London, 1838

This African species was drawn and lithographed by Gould and his wife
and retains more of the fresh quality of their originals than most of those
lithographed by other hands.

Trogons are found in both the New and the Old World. They are
amongst the most gaily plumaged of all birds and include the
spectacular Quetzal (Plate 98) amongst their members. The Narina
Trogon lives on the banks of the River Gamtoos. During the mating
season the male utters a melancholy cry but the rest of the year is silent.

Lithograph, 21 × 14 in. (533 × 356 mm.)

TROGON NARINA, (Shaw)
Narina Trogon.

TAB. III.

Fig. 2.

Fig. 1.

A. *Schouman del. ad viv.*

I.F. *Schuster sc. Berolini.*

TAB. I.

C. *Hiller delin.*

C. B. *Glassbach sc.*

104, 105

Manakin *(Chiroxiphia* sp.*)*
Tufted Puffin *(Lunda cirrhata)*

Plates 3 and 1 from Fasc. 5 of *Spicilegia Zoologica*, by P. S. Pallas,
Berlin, 1769

In the eighteenth century men of outstanding ability were able to make
valuable contributions to several different sciences on a scale which we
can scarcely realize today, when there is so much pressure on men and
women to specialize from an early age. Peter Simon Pallas (1741–1811)
was one of these gifted polymaths. Born in Berlin, he studied medicine
there, then at Halle, Göttingen and Leyden. Afterwards he spent several
years in Holland working on tropical collections. He also visited England
to examine coastal geology. Later he was invited by the Empress Catherine
to visit Russia to participate as naturalist in an expedition to observe
the 1769 Transit of Venus. He spent six years travelling across Russia
and Siberia, examining the geology of various mountain ranges and
collecting animals.

He discovered the Yenesei Meteorite on this journey, and enormous
fossil deposits of elephants, mammoths and other large mammals. His
ideas on mountain building were greatly in advance of the theories current
at that time. He also made a profound study of the anatomy, morphology
and habits of the rodents he had collected. This was the best work then
available on the structure of an entire order and paved the way for
modern studies on comparative anatomy. He retired to the Crimea and
devoted himself largely to botanical work. In 1810, after the death of his
second wife, he returned to Berlin where he died a year later.

Males of some species of *Chiroxiphia*, a South American genus,
collaborate in formal courtship dances before the female, taking turns to
occupy the key position in the display.

Tufted Puffins are birds of the North Pacific. Many puffins have
brightly coloured plates on the bill during the breeding season, and shed
them during the moult.

Engravings, each approximately 7·5 × 6 in. (190 × 153 mm.)

106, 107, 108, 109
Owl, Toucan, Spoonbill and Pelican

Plates 19, 31, 71 and 77 from *The History of Birds . . .*, anonymous,
London, 1791

The only bird that can be identified with certainty amongst the four
selected from this early example of a natural history book for children
is the Spoonbill (*Platalea leucorodia*) which still breeds in the Netherlands.
Although there are a few earlier examples of children's books going back
to the sixteenth century, it was not until the eighteenth century that
improving books and simple story tales designed for young people began
to make their appearance; they seem to have coincided with the
establishment of large numbers of schools by private donors for the
children of the labouring and artisan classes, and it is pleasant to realize
that some were quite light-hearted, such as this one from which these
woodcuts were chosen.

Woodcuts, 3·95 × 3·1 in. (100 × 80 mm.)

The OWL

THE grave Owl with wisdom fraught
In sober solemn Silence sits.

The OWL is a Bird of the night and is in a constant Enmity with those who love the Light and sing in the day. It lives on vermin, and particularly on mice: they commonly dwell in trunks of hollow trees, or in old Ruins and deserted Places, neither frequented by Man nor any other Birds besides themselves. For if he happens to be discovered by any other of the feathered Race, he is sure of being beat and stripped of all his Plumage.

The TOUCAN.

THE Toucan presents you
A branch in his claw;
And a wonderful head,
With a Bill like a Saw.

31

The TOUCAN-PIE is about the size of the Jackdaw. Its Bill is reported to be prodigiously thick, and almost as long as its whole body. Its Head is large and formed to support a Bill of such extraordinary bulk. The Head, Neck and Wings are black; the Breast near the Neck tinged with red, which a little lower changes into bright and shining gold coulour; the Belly & thighs are of a beautiful vermilion, and the Tail black tipped with a lovely red.   B 4

The SPOON-BILL

THE Spoon-bills, they in droves,
Frequent the silent shady groves.

(71)

The SPOON-BILL derives its name from the shape of its bill, which resembles a spoon. It is a very large Bird, and has its whole body perfectly white, like a Swan's. It builds on the tops of high trees, in a wood, near a village called Lavenhuys, not from Leyden in Holland.

The PELICAN

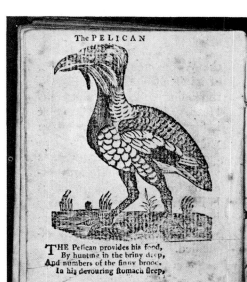

THE Pelican provides his food,
By hunting in the briny deep,
And numbers of the finny brood,
In his devouring stomach sleep.

(77)

The PELICAN is a very large Sea-fowl. being nearly as big as the Swan, its whole body is white. It differs from other Birds in having a large bag hanging down from its Bill. This bag it sometimes contracts and draws up, so that it is scarce to be seen, and at other times suffers it to be swelled to such a degree, as to contain a very large quantity of water. It feeds upon fish, and is said to live to a great age.

D 3

13.

FALCO CANDICANS, *J.F. Gmel.*

J. Wolf & H.C. Richter, del. et lith.

Greenland Falcon, light race adult and young

Walter Imp.

Greenland Falcon *(Falco rusticolus candicans)*

Plate 13 from *The Birds of Great Britain*, by John Gould, Vol. 1, London, 1863 [1862]–73

This painting of the light race of the Greenland Falcon is by J. Wolf (1820–99), one of the most sought-after of the bird painters of the nineteenth century. He carried out many commissions for Gould but there does not appear to have been a good relationship between them. Gould (1804–81) was immensely energetic, and was probably driven to overcompensate for the struggles of his early life.

Greenland Falcons were in great demand during the Middle Ages, and were often a part, sometimes the whole, of a 'King's Ransom'. They do not breed in the British Isles but occur as visitors.

Lithograph, 19 × 14 in. (483 × 356 mm.)

111

Common Grey Hornbill *(Tockus birostris)*

Plate 45 from Vol. 2 of unpublished drawings by Indian artists, 1820–58, Hodgson Collection, Zoological Society, London

Brian Houghton Hodgson (1800–94) was a civil servant in the East India Company with the same training and background as Christopher Webb-Smith (Plate 125) who was seven years older, Both men spent some years at the East India College which became Haileybury, and it seems probable that it was there, under Professor Walter, that they acquired the interest and training in biology that enabled them both to make very considerable contributions to ornithology. Hodgson was more gifted in some ways than Webb-Smith but he appears to have had little talent as a draughtsman; the remarkable series of ornithological drawings and paintings bearing his name, in the library of the Zoological Society of London, is the work of at least three Indian artists who worked for him. The Sanscrit phrase refers not to the artist but to the locality where this species was found: 'Always in central Veighai.'

He was a man of immense intellectual capacity and carried out valuable researches in comparative Indo-Chinese philology, as well as in the physical geography of Nepal and Tibet and the zoology of the regions where so much of his life was spent.

In India he became a close friend of Sir Charles D'Oyly (Plate 126) and his wife; it is probable that the lightly sketched backgrounds that feature in so many of his artists' drawings were the result of the similar treatment of the plates in *Oriental Ornithology* published jointly by Webb-Smith and D'Oyly in 1829. Among his other notable friends were Alexander Humboldt (Plate 87) and Sir Joseph Hooker.

Hodgson wrote over one hundred and twenty-seven papers on natural history subjects, and made a collection of 9,512 bird skins. Among them was the first specimen of the Tibetan Eared Pheasant (Plate 120).

Hornbills are common Asiatic birds. For a note on another species see Plate 131.

Watercolour and pencil, 12·3 × 19·25 in. (310 × 490 mm.)

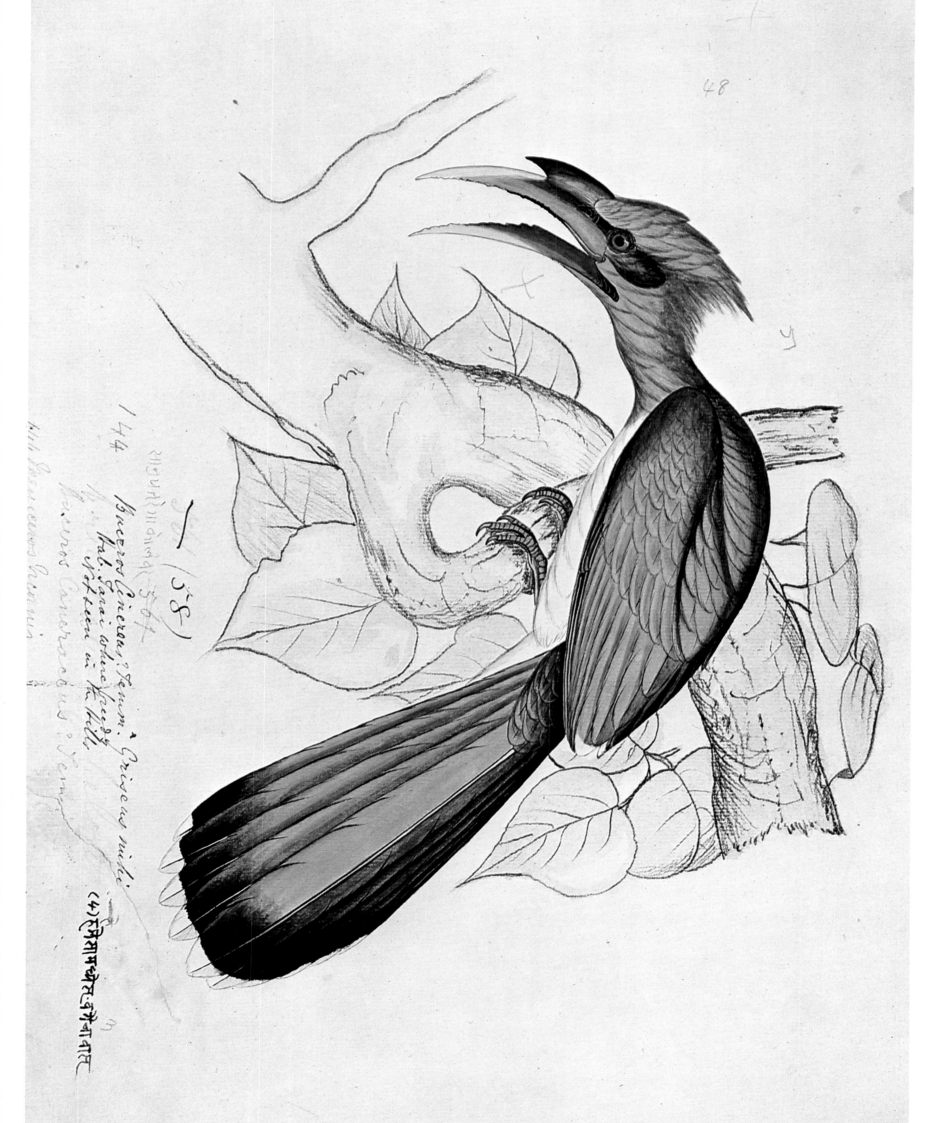

48

144. Buceros Cinereus? Temm. Griseus mihi
Hab: Javai where breeds
Natives in the hills

Buceros Canencadus? Temm.

Hab: Buceros Pearcei

(4) डोस्नाम्बवेलगोगेनार

—J (58)

राधुराभाटाचार्य 5 द.

THE RING DOTTEREL.
RING PLOVER, OR SEA LARK.

(Charadrius Hiaticula, Lin.—Le petit Pluvier à collier, Buff.)

THE MARSH TITMOUSE.
BLACK-CAPPED TITMOUSE.

(Parus, paluſtris, Lin.—Le Meſange de marais, Buff.)

THE PIED WAGTAIL.
BLACK AND WHITE WATER-WAGTAIL.

(Motacilla Alba, Lin.—La Lavandiere, Buff.)

GREATER SPOTTED WOODPECKER.
WITWALL.

(Picus Major, Lin.—L'Epeiche, ou le Pic varie, Buff.)

THE REDBREAST.
ROBIN-REDBREAST, OR RUDDOCK.

(Motacilla rubecola, Lin.—Le Rouge-gorge, Buff.)

THE SKYLARK.
LAVROCK.

(Alauda arvenſis, Lin.—L'Alouette, Buff.)

112, 113, 114, 115, 116, 117

Various birds

Plates from pages 119, 90, 68, 46, 74 and 65 of *Figures of British Land Birds engraved on wood by T. Bewick*, Newcastle-on-Tyne, 1800

A countryman and naturalist at heart, Bewick (1753–1828) equipped himself so well, during his apprenticeship to an engraver in Newcastle-on-Tyne, that his illustrations probably inspired more young naturalists than the work of any other artist at the close of the eighteenth century. He was born in Northumberland, and was known at school for the embellishments to his exercises rather for their content. His first published wood engravings appeared in articles by the mathematician Charles Hutton in *The Ladies' Diary*; they show that he was experimenting with wood engraving very early in his apprenticeship which he entered at the age of fourteen. He reinvigorated the art of printing from wood by cutting across the end of the block instead of along it, and by reversing the standard process so that what he cut away was more important than what was left on the block.

The birds shown here are Ringed Plover (*Charadrius hiaticula*), Marsh Tit (*Parus palustris*), Pied Wagtail (*Motacilla alba*), Great Spotted Woodpecker (*Dryobates major*), Robin (*Erithacus rubecula*) and Skylark (*Alauda arvensis*).

Wood engravings, each approximately 3 × 4 in. (76 × 102 mm.)

118, 119

Various birds

Plates 46 and 44 from *The Hokusai Sketch Books*, by James A. Michener, published by Charles E. Tuttle Co., Inc., Tokyo, 1960

These two pages of drawings by Hokusai Katsushika (1760–1849) are taken from a recent edition of the Manga Sketchbooks. Manga is an old word meaning ten thousand pictures; it has changed its meaning and is now applied to strip cartoons. The sketchbooks contain many hundreds of drawings depicting plants, animals, human beings, landscapes, clouds, fables etc. They were intended for publication and were never merely an artist's jottings.

At the age of eighteen Hokusai entered the studio of Katsugawa Shunsho, a painter and designer of considerable importance. The younger man was impatient with the principles of his master and his disregard of them led to his explusion from the school in 1785. Hokusai had something of the prodigious vitality of Turner. His output was enormous but in spite of his popularity in his own country he remained poor throughout his life. The saying so often quoted as his dying utterance (pp. 21–2): 'If Heaven had lent me but five years more I should have become a great painter'–occurs on the colophon of one of his books.

Pen and wash drawings, each $7 \times 4 \cdot 8$ in. (178×123 mm.)

J Wolf & J Smit del et lith.

M & N Hanhart imp.

CROSSOPTILON DROUYNII.

120

Eared or Snow Pheasant (*Crossoptilon crossoptilon*)

Plate 15 from *A Monograph of the Phasianidae . . .*, by D. G. Elliot,
Vol. 1, New York, 1872

This volume is dedicated to Joseph Wolf, the painter of this plate, in the
following words: 'To Joseph Wolf, Esq., F.Z.S., etc. whose unrivalled
talent has graced this work with its chief attraction and whose
marvellous power of delineating animal life renders him unequalled in our
time.' Plates 121 and 124 are also by Wolf.

There are various races of Eared Pheasant. The first to be described
was taken to B. H. Hodgson (Plates 111, 140) at Katmandu, by a
Nepalese envoy to China; the place of its capture is unknown. Most forms
live in Tibet or the mountains of western and northern China.

D. G. Elliot (1835–1915) was a wealthy American, Curator of
Zoology at the Field Museum, Chicago. He wrote sumptuous
ornithological books, the best known of which are these volumes on the
pheasants, and another set on birds of paradise. The latter was dedicated
to Alfred Russell Wallace (Plate 130), and illustrated by Wolf; a
monograph by Bowdler Sharpe (1847–1909) on the same group of birds
(Plates 138, 139), illustrated by W. Hart and published more than
twenty years later, was more comprehensive.

Lithograph, 16 × 19 in. (407 × 485 mm.)

121

Elliot's Pheasant *(Calophasis ellioti)*

Plate 13 *bis* from *A Monograph of the Phasianidae . . .*, by D. G. Elliot, Vol. 2, New York, 1872

There are sixteen genera of pheasants, many species of which are spectacularly beautiful (see also Plate 120). Most of them live in the mountains of Asia but a few occur at lower altitudes in Malaysia. Elliot's Pheasant comes from the mountains behind Ningpo in Chekiang.

Lithograph, 23·5 × 18 in. (597 × 457 mm.)

122
OVERLEAF

Black-bellied Darter *(Anhinga melanogaster)*
Cormorant *(Phalacrocorax ?fuscicollis)*

Plate 74 from Vol. 3 of the Wellesley Collection, by an unknown Indian artist, Calcutta, *c.* 1800, India Office Library, London

Darters or Snake-birds are widely distributed in the Americas, Asia, Africa and parts of Australasia. They frequent tropical and subtropical inland waters and are immensely active underwater swimmers. When they come to the surface they do so in such a way that only the long neck and head are visible, hence the popular name, though in fact they almost equally resemble the crooked stems and buds of water lilies; they certainly present a very odd appearance seen from a distance. The vertebrae are curiously modified, the first seven cervicals forming a continuous curve, concave in front, while the eighth articulates with the seventh almost at right angles. For a note on the Wellesley Collection see Plate 59.

Watercolour, 19·5 × 12·15 in. (495 × 310 mm.)

123
OVERLEAF

Hen Harriers *(Circus cyaneus)*

Plate 10 from *Illustrations of British Ornithology*, by P. J. Selby, Edinburgh and London, 1821

This portrait of a male and female Hen Harrier shows the difference in size between the sexes, the male being the smaller grey-and-white bird in the foreground; the female is much larger and has more elaborately marked brown-and-buff plumage. These birds rarely breed in England now, but they still nest in Orkney and some of the Outer Hebrides.

Selby (1788–1867) worked on the same scale as Audubon, and many of his birds (though not these Hen Harriers) are painted life-size. He is best known for his collaboration with W. Jardine in the ornithological volumes of *The Naturalist's Library*. Some accounts of his work ascribe the plates in *Illustrations of British Ornithology* to original designs by Edward Lear, but as Lear was born in 1812 this cannot be the case.

Engraving, 21 × 16·25 in. (533 × 413 mm.)

13. bis.

CALOPHASIS ELLIOTI

124

Shoebills *(Balaeniceps rex)*

Folio 84 from Vol. 5 of *Aves*, by Joseph Wolf, unpublished, Zoological Society, London

These birds are sometimes called Whale-headed or Shoe-billed Storks, but in fact it seems doubtful that they belong to the order Ciconiiformes. Some anatomists consider that they are most closely allied to the pelicans, but in any case they are agreed to be the only member of the family Balaenicipitidae.

They are large birds, three-and-a-half feet high, and are found in swampy areas of tropical eastern Africa. They spend a good deal of time standing about waiting for the fish and other creatures on which they live to come within reach. The huge bill has a small hook at the end and is thought possibly to be useful in digging up the mudfish which form part of their diet.

Joseph Wolf (1820–99), who painted this group of Shoebills, was one of the most sought-after animal painters of the nineteenth century, and is represented by two other paintings in this volume (Plates 120, 121).

Watercolour, 9·5 × 13·3 in. (241 × 339 mm.)

125

Cinnamon Dove *(Aplopelia larvata)*

Plate XIX from *Birds, Flowers and Scenery of the Cape of Good Hope*, by Christopher Webb-Smith, unpublished, 1839–59, Balfour Library, Cambridge

Christopher Webb-Smith (1793–1871) was born at Camberwell and educated at the East India Company Training College which later became Haileybury. Here he studied Bengalee and then moved to Fitzwilliam College at Calcutta. After completing a course there he was appointed to the magistracy at Bihar where he began to make careful studies of Indian birds. He was greatly influenced by Bewick's *British Birds* (Plates 112–117) which he had owned as a child. He then collaborated with Sir Charles D'Oyly, another Indian civil servant to whom he was related by marriage, and together they produced a small illustrated book on Indian birds, in which Sir Charles drew the backgrounds and Webb-Smith the birds. These were lithographed and printed at their own press run by 'The United Patna and Gizar Society or Behar School of Athens, for the promotion of Arts and Science, and for the circulation of fun and merriment of all descriptions'.

Two of these volumes, *The Feathered Game of Hindostan* (1828) and *Oriental Ornithology* (1829), were the first British books in which lithography was used for bird illustration (The earliest Continental lithographs were those by Langlumé and others, after drawings by J. C. Werner, in the *Atlas des Oiseaux d'Europe*, 1826–40.)

In 1837 Webb-Smith moved to the Cape of Good Hope where he set to work to paint the birds and plants; the birds were drawn half-size and it is from a volume of these watercolours that this plate is taken. He eventually retired to Florence where he died in 1871.

Watercolour, 22 × 18·25 in. (561 × 462 mm.)

XIX.

CWSmith Ornith.

C. D'Oyly delt. B.: Jany. 1831.

126

Bishop or Woolly-necked Stork *(Dissoura episcopus)*

Folio 258 from *Indian Birds and Scenery*, by C. Webb-Smith and Charles D'Oyly, unpublished, *c.* 1829–59, Balfour Library, Cambridge

The story of the collaboration between C. Webb-Smith and Sir Charles D'Oyly is discussed in the note to Plate 125. In many cases D'Oyly left his landscapes uncoloured while the birds were painted in bright colours by his friend. This plate is interesting in the combination of painting techniques by both men. They were among the first to use lithography for ornithological illustration. D'Oyly was also a close friend of B. H. Hodgson (Plates 111, 120, 140) whose Indian artists simulated a lithographic technique by painting birds against a background of black-and-white outlines.

There is little doubt that this plate represents a Bishop Stork; the name Undertaker (below the painting) is applied to the Adjutant Stork *(Leptoptilos dubius)* which possesses a pouch, not a ruff, and is a useful scavenger. Bishop Storks are found in India, Africa and Malaysia.

Watercolour, 21 × 18 in. (533 × 457 mm.)

127

Ivory-billed Woodpecker *(Campephilus principalis)*

Plate 109 from *Histoire Naturelle des Oiseaux de l'Amérique Septentrionale* . . ., by L. J. P. Vieillot, Vol. 2, Paris, 1807

The Ivory-billed Woodpecker is the largest woodpecker known to science. It used to range from Central America and Mexico north to Pennsylvania, but is now almost or quite extinct. Its Mexican name was the Carpenter since it had a bill three inches long which it used to dig out a spiral nesting burrow, thought perhaps to give the young more shelter from the weather. These woodpeckers are black and white but the male has a brilliant scarlet crest and is a marvellously handsome bird.

Louis Jean Pierre Vieillot (1748–1831) was one of the pioneers with Alexander Wilson (Plate 88) of a new kind of ornithology in which birds were no longer amassed merely as specimens but studied as living organisms, with careful observations of their life-histories and types of behaviour. Vieillot paid particular attention to the variations of plumage in any one species at different stages of its life-cycle. He was born at Yvetot, France, and worked in Paris as a clerk for a time, studying birds meanwhile. But he felt that he would have better opportunities abroad, so emigrated with his family to Santo Domingo, and thence to the United States. He was very gifted, and accomplished much solid work, but was always overshadowed by the brilliance of his contemporaries such as Buffon (Plates 79, 80) and Cuvier (Plate 136).

Engraving, 14·1 × 10·8 in. (358 × 275 mm.)

Le Pic noir à bec blanc. Picus principalis. *L.n. g.* pl. 109

Victor Paul.   Langlois imp.   Bouquet Sculp.

128

Blue Penguin *(Eudyptula minor)*

Folio 42 from *Notes and Drawings* . . ., by R. Laishley, unpublished,
c. 1863–83, British Museum (Natural History)

Laishley appears to have been rather a melancholy amateur naturalist
who went from England to New Zealand in the second part of the
nineteenth century. According to the manuscript that accompanies his
book of drawings, he lived at Onehunga, near Auckland, for a number of
years. Many of his notes on the birds and insects of New Zealand are
copied from published sources but there are a few interesting observations,
as for, instance, some details about Australian White-eyes *(Zosterops
lateralis)* in the early years of their colonization of New Zealand.

Laishley has successfully shown the texture of the penguins' plumage.
These birds spend much time oiling and preening their feathers as these
form an essential protection against the cold waters of the southern
oceans in which penguins spend most of their lives. They come on shore
only during the breeding and moulting periods. At those times Blue
Penguins may be seen on many parts of the New Zealand coast. This
group may well have been painted on the outskirts of Wellington with a
southerly storm blowing up.

Watercolour, 18·25 × 15·3 in. (465 × 285 mm.)

129

Frogmouth *(Batrachostomus auritas)*
Plate 17 from *Icones Avium*, by John Gould, part 2, London, 1838

This plate, like that of the Narina Trogon (Plate 103) was 'drawn from nature and on stone by J. and E. Gould' and is a fine example of the joint work of these two artists. Gould coined the word 'frogmouth' for this genus of nightjars, which, together with *Podargus*, comprise a family confined to the Oriental and Australasian regions. They resemble the true nightjars in their plumage and in some structural characters, but differ considerably in others. Their huge mouths led naturalists to believe that they were wonderfully adapted for catching nocturnal insects on the wing, but this is not so; most of their food consists of insects and other small invertebrates, sometimes small birds and rodents, most of which are taken on the ground.

Batrachostomus makes a flattened kind of nest out of its own down, with a layer of spiderweb and lichen on the outside. Gould knew nothing of the habits of the handsome pair he drew; he seems to have taken his few notes from the appendix to Lady Raffles's *Memoir* to her husband, the famous founder of Singapore. Sir Stamford Raffles amassed a vast collection of Oriental manuscripts, plants and animals during his time in Malaysia. Like Wallace on leaving the Amazon (see Plates 130, 131) he lost them all in a fire at sea on his way back to England. *Rafflesia* was named after him, an ambivalent compliment; it is parasitic and has the largest flower in the world, but it smells of carrion.

Lithograph, 20 × 13 in. (510 × 331 mm.)

BATRÁCHOSTOMUS AURITUS; (Gould)

Drawn from Nature & on Stone by J. & E. Gould.   Printed by C. Hullmandel.

130, 131

Great Bird of Paradise *(Paradisea apoda)*
Great Indian Hornbill *(Buceros bicornis)*

Plates 34 and 18 from *The Malay Archipelago . . .*, by Alfred Russell
Wallace, London, 1869

Alfred Russell Wallace was one of the small group of nineteenth-century
naturalists for whom the rich variety of plants and animals of South
America provided a remarkable stimulus. Among others were Alexander
von Humboldt (Plate 87), Charles Darwin, H. W. Bates and Richard
Spruce.

Bates and Wallace made friends as young men. Passionately interested
in natural history, and highly intelligent, they realized that with their
relatively humble backgrounds they were unlikely to earn a living as
biologists unless they were also collectors, so they decided to establish
themselves on the Amazon. After two years there Wallace moved to the
Malay archipelago where he travelled widely. There he worked out a
theory of natural selection as the chief means of evolution which he sent to
Darwin who found that it exactly paralleled his own ideas. Darwin was
persuaded by his colleagues to publish independently, but both men
behaved generously and remained firm friends. Wallace's account of his
wanderings in the Malayan islands is one of the great classics of natural
history.

Hornbills and most of the birds of paradise have very different types of
behaviour as regards incubation and the care of the young. The female
hornbill lays her eggs in a hole or hollow of a tree, then walls herself with
mud and dung, assisted by the male who thereafter brings her food
which he passes through a slit. In some species he has been observed to
bring her flowers as well as fruit and berries. The incubation and
fledgeling periods may last for a hundred days or more and in some
species the female remains immured for the whole of this time. In some
cases she keeps the nest clean by defecating at high velocity through the
slit in the wall.

The state of affairs is very different in many birds of paradise. The
Great Bird of Paradise, illustrated here, is a fruit eater. Breeding takes
place when there are abundant supplies and the inconspicuous female is
able to look after the young unaided. With time to spare, the males have
evolved the brilliant and elaborate variation of plumage which has made
them so attractive to man. When the breeding plumage is fully developed.
they gather in large groups, or leks, on certain trees where they perform
ritual dances which are highly elaborate and appear to induce a state of
trance. The most favoured trees become known to the hunters who build
shelters at the base, from which they can shoot the birds with great ease.
The females attend these displays and select their mates before retiring
to their long period of domestic duties.

Both these engravings were from drawings by T. W. Wood, who
probably had sketches by Wallace to work from.

Engravings, 5·65 × 3·7 in. (143 × 95 mm.) and 4·5 × 3·5 in. (114 × 89 mm.)

132, 133
Scops Owl *(Otus scops)*
Cuckoo *(Cuculus canorus)*

Plates 1 and 3 from Heft 2 of *Abbildungen aus dem Thierreiche . . .
Ornithologie*, by J. C. Susemihl, Darmstadt, 1821–6

J. C. Susemihl (1767–1837), a Hessian draughtsman and engraver,
worked with members of his family on zoological illustration. This lively
representation of a Scops Owl is one of his most appealing engravings.
The cuckoo, too, has been carefully observed and shows what a
remarkable advance in technique had been achieved since the engraved
portrait of a cuckoo by Olina (Plate 72, 1622) just two centuries earlier.

Engravings, 7·85 × 10·25 in. (200 × 260 mm.) and 7·85 × 10·65 in.
(200 × 270 mm.)

Strix otus. Linn: mas:

C. Susemihl pinx.& sc.

C. Susemihl fec.

III

Cuculus canorus. Linn: mas:

134

Racquet-tailed Kingfisher *(Tanysiptera vulcani)*

Folio 12 from Vol. 3 of *Alcedinae*, by Henry Jones, unpublished, *c.* 1900, Zoological Society, London

Major Henry Jones (1838–1921) is an almost unknown bird painter of great skill. Born near Folkestone, he joined the army as an ensign when he was twenty-two years old, and served under Lord Napier. He retired when he was forty-three, after serving in India for fifteen years. Nothing appears to be known of his training as an artist but it seems probable that he learnt much during his time in India where so many other army officers were interested in depicting the birds of that country. After retirement he became a constant visitor to the Bird Room of the British Museum and painted a great number of the specimens there, carefully noting the provenance of each one so that the forty-three unpublished folio volumes of his work constitute a valuable record of specimens collected by many famous naturalists of the nineteenth century. All these birds are figured in their natural surroundings and possess a vitality that is surprising to anyone familiar with a collection almost entirely composed of dried skins.

Racquet-tailed Kingfishers are confined to the Moluccas, New Guinea and the extreme north of Australia. They live on insects and other small invertebrates.

Watercolour, 14·4 × 10·45 in. (371 × 264 mm.)

135

Kakapo or Owl Parrot *(Strigops habroptilus)*

Plate 57 from the *Supplement to the Birds of Australia*, by John Gould, London, 1869

The Kakapo used to be widely distributed throughout New Zealand but, as it is unable to fly, it was easily hunted and is almost extinct. This painting by Gould is little known since the volume in which it appears has no reference to New Zealand birds in the title. Amongst other interesting birds from that country which it figures is *Sceloglaux albifacies*, the Whekau, an owl that is also approaching extinction.

In the middle of the last century the Kakapos lived in colonies and formed their own pathways which made it easy to pursue and catch them. Sir George Grey sent Gould notes on these birds which Gould published:

> About sunset it comes forth from its retreat, and feeds on grass, weeds, vegetables, fruits, deeds and roots. It . . . only uses its short wings for the purpose of aiding its progress when running, balancing itself when on a tree, or in making a short descent, half-jump, half-flight from a higher to a lower bough . . .
>
> The Kakapo is a very clever and intelligent bird, in fact singularly so; contracts a strong affection for those who are kind to it, shows its attachment by climbing about and rubbing itself against its friend . . ., in fact were it not for its dirty habits more than any other bird with which I am acquainted; for its method of showing its attachment by playfulness and fondling, is more like that of a dog than a bird.

Lithograph, $21\cdot4 \times 14\cdot5$ in. (545×368 mm.)

136
OVERLEAF

Ostrich *(Struthio camelus)*

Plate [4] from *Le Ménagerie du Muséum National d'Histoire Naturelle . . .*, by Lacépède and Cuvier, Paris 1801

One gets the feeling that Lacépède and Cuvier very much enjoyed poking fun at accepted authorities since they quote opposing statements without comment; Buffon, they say, regarded ostriches as extremely lascivious, whereas Thévenot (1633–67) considered them to be models of conjugal stability.

Ostriches used to be commonly distributed throughout Africa, particularly in sandy and relatively desert areas but they are also found in open woodland. One of the tribes in Ethiopia were formerly known as Struthiophages because they lived largely on these birds. Arabs enjoy a special dish made from the coagulated blood and fat of ostriches.

Lacépède and Cuvier also point out that the ostrich was one of the animals known from the earliest records, and that there are accounts of it both in Herodotus (about 484–425 BC) and Job whose great poem may antedate Herodotus:

> *Gavest thou the goodly wings unto the peacocks? or wings and feathers unto the ostrich? Who leaveth her eggs in the earth and warmeth them in the dust, And forgetteth that the foot may crush them, or that the wild beast may break them . . . What time she lifteth up herself on high, she scorneth the horse and his rider.*

Although ostriches are flightless the wings help with their locomotion, just as the old prophet remarked; chicks of only one month old can run at a speed of thirty-five miles an hour. Unfortunately these great birds, some of which stand eight feet high, are unable to escape from fast cars and their numbers have been greatly reduced in the last few decades.

Engraving, $12 \times 9\cdot6$ in. (245×357 mm.)

57.

STRIGOPS HABROPTILUS, *G. R. Gray.*

J. Gould & H. C. Richter, del. et lith.

Hullmandel & Walton, Imp.

Peinte par Maréchal. *Niger.* *Gravée par Miger.*

STRUTHIO CAMELUS (*Femina*)   L'AUTRUCHE FEMELE.

Sixieme de la Grandeur.

TRICHOPARADISEA GULIELMI (*Cab.*)

W. Hart del. et lith.

Mintern Bros. imp.

137

ON PREVIOUS PAGE

One-wattled Cassowary *(Casuarius uniappendiculatus)*

Folio 15 from Folder 3 of the W. B. Rothschild Collection, British Museum (Natural History)

This cassowary comes from Salawatty Island and the adjoining region of north-west New Guinea. It was described in 1860 by Blyth from a bird in a menagerie in Calcutta; shortly afterwards a specimen was obtained for the Amsterdam Zoological Gardens. Gould heard of it and managed to get a drawing from Robert Kretschmar of Leipzig. From this he and Richter prepared an illustration which was published in his *Supplement to the Birds of Australia* (1869). The unpublished drawing reproduced here was executed by T. G. Keulemans for Lord Rothschild but was not included in his monograph of *Casuarius* (1901).

Watercolour, 15·7 × 9·8 in. (405 × 250 mm.)

138

Emperor of Germany's Bird of Paradise *(Paradisea gulielmi)*

Plate 27 from *Monograph of the Paradiseidae . . . and Ptilonothynicidae . . .,* by R. Bowdler Sharpe, Vol. 1, London, 1891–8

This bird of paradise was discovered in New Guinea rather later than the others figured in this book (Plates 75, 139). Forms resembling it were however among the earliest to be traded in the East Indies, and, since the wings and feet were removed to enable them to be dried more successfully, the idea that they had a way of life fundamentally different from that of other birds gained credence in the West.

One of the earliest descriptions of any bird of paradise to appear in English was a translation in 1598 of an account, which contained this myth, by the Dutch traveller and author, Jan Huyghen van Linschoten (1563–1611). The following passage is taken from the Hakluyt Society reprint of 1885:

> In these Ilands onlie is found the bird which the Portingales call Passaros de Sol, that is Fowle of the Sunne, . . . by us called Paradice birdes, for ye beauty of their feathers which passe all other birdes . . . They flie, as it is said, alwaies into the Sunne, and keepe themselves continually in the ayre, without alighting on the earth, for they have neither feet nor wings, but only head and body, and the most part tayle, as appeareth by the birdes that are brought from thence into India, and some from thence hether, but not many for they are costlie.

Lithograph, by W. Hart, 21 × 13·8 in. (533 × 352 mm.)

139

Black Sickle-billed Bird of Paradise *(Epimachus fastuosus)*

Plate 14 from *Monograph of the Paradiseidae . . . and Ptilonothynicidae . . .*, by R. Bowdler Sharpe, Vol. 1, London, 1891–8

This bird of paradise was first described by Valentijn (Plate 75). It comes from the mountains of north-west New Guinea, and is believed to nest on the ground, preferably in hollows under rocks where there are two exits. In fact little appears to be known about its habits. Its elaborate plumage meant that it was hunted by natives and used as an article of trade in the sixteenth century and probably much earlier. It was called the Grand Promerops by Pennant (Plates 89, 90, 101) and others; Pennant gave a good account of it in the second edition of *Indian Zoology* (1790):

> The larger variety of these is sold by the natives without wings or feet and therefore is very difficult to be described with accuracy. The remains are generally stretched out on a stick to the length of four spans. The feathers of the head, neck, and belly are black, silky and mixed with a radiant hue or purple and gold . . . The birds of this variety are brought only from the part of *New Guinea* called *Serghile*. The inhabitants carry the skins dried upon sticks by smoke, and enclosed in bamboo joints to the island *Salawat*, and exchange them for hatchets and coarse cloths. . . . In *Ternate* and *Tidore* they are called *Softu-kokotu*, Black Paradise Birds.

Lithograph, by W. Hart, 21 × 13·8 in. (533 × 352 mm.)

EPIMACHUS SPECIOSUS, (Bodd.)

W. Hart. del. et. lith.

Mintern Bros. imp.

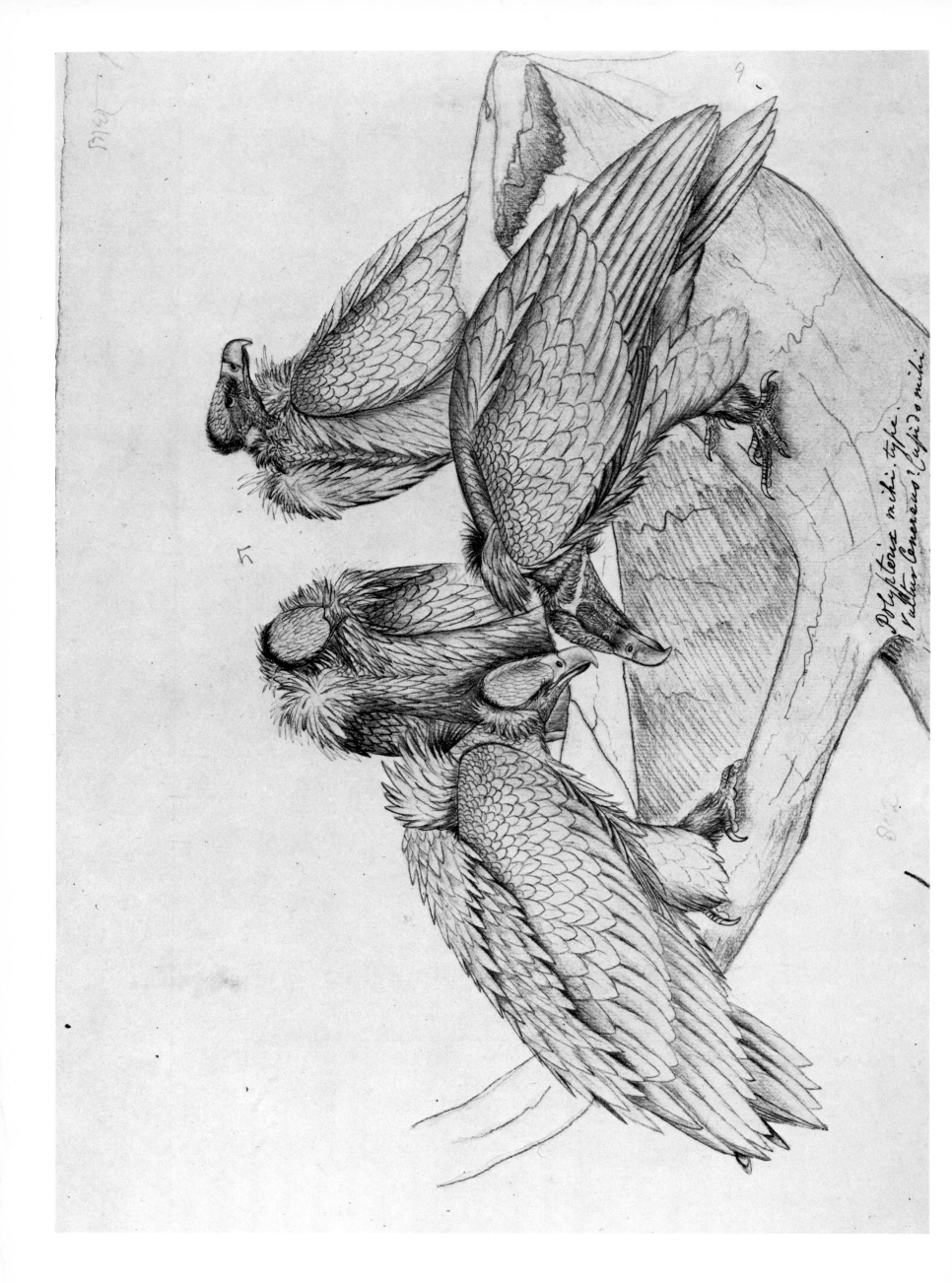

140

Black or Cinereous Vulture *(Aegypius monachus)*

Plate 6 in Vol. 1 of unpublished drawings by Indian artists, 1820–58,
Hodgson Collection, Zoological Society, London

Nothing appears to be known of the Indian artist who drew this and many
other bird studies for B. H. Hodgson (Plate 111). He seems to have had a
special aptitude for birds of prey and some of his studies of owls are
magnificent. These drawings are of particular interest in that many of
them are surrounded by carefully observed details of claws, eyes and bills,
and even dissections. It is probable that the name of this man and some of
the other artists who worked for Hodgson might be found in family
correspondence, and it is to be hoped that someone will attempt this
task before too long so that the drawings will become better known.

Vultures find their prey by sight rather than smell and it is well known
how quickly a group will gather apparently from a clear sky, round a
dead animal. There is no doubt that they have a highly developed sense of
smell in addition and it is possible that this may operate in some fashion
analogous to the way in which male moths of some species are attracted
from great distances to the wingless females.

Pencil drawing, 12·15 × 19·25 in. (310 × 490 mm.)

141

Black Guillemot or Tystie *(Cepphus grylle)*

Plate VI from *Birds drawn from nature*, by Mrs Hugh Blackburn, Glasgow, 1868

Mrs Blackburn drew the living birds either in the field or in brief captivity. Of this bird she wrote: 'The bird was caught alive on her eggs on a little rocky island at the mouth of Loch Ailort, where a few pairs breed annually. She returned to her eggs—one cannot call it her nest—after her picture had been taken.'

She seems to have realized how much was lost in the ordinary processes of reproduction at that time and gave this note on her methods in the introduction:

In order to carry out the same idea of interposing as few interpreters as possible between nature and the actual print, the drawings have been copied on to the stone (or zinc plate) by the same hand as made the original drawings, or in some instances the drawing has been made on the stone direct from nature.

Lithograph, 10 × 11 in. (255 × 366 mm.)

142

Manchurian Crane *(Grus japonensis)*

Painting by Haruki Nammei, Department of Oriental Antiquities,
British Museum

This is a typical academic painting connected with the restoration of the
Japanese monarchy of 1867. Haruki Nammei (1795–1878) was an eclectic,
painting in many styles, generally more sensitive than this, although the
crane is beautifully observed. The rising sun is the Imperialist symbol.
Unaware of the meaning of the painting, I chose it because I thought
that the sun was setting, and the bird coming to rest on the waves, so
that it was an appropriate subject with which to end this book. It was
only when the book was almost ready for the press, and the blocks for the
illustrations processed, that I learnt the truth of the symbolism. To me the
feeling of the painting is still one of sunset and I hope that perhaps the
owners of this volume will come to regard it in the same way.

Ink and colours on paper, 63·75 × 33·5 in. (1,620 × 850 mm.)

Bibliography

Works cited

Books from which illustrations have been reproduced are followed by plate numbers

ALBERTUS MAGNUS (Saint Albert, surnamed the Great, Bishop of Ratisbon). *Boke of secretes of Albartus Magnus, of the virtues of Herbes, stones and certaine beastes . . .*, London, 1525

ALBIN, E. *Natural History of Birds*, London, 1731–8

— *Histoire Naturelle des Oiseaux ornée de 306 Estampes*, The Hague, 1750 (23)

ALDROVANDI, U. *Ornithologiae hoc est de Avibus historiae Libri XII*, Frankfurt, 1610 (50)

— *Ornithologiae hoc est de Avibus historiae Libri XII . . .*, Bologna, 1637–46 (33, 34, 47, 51)

— *Ornithologiae Tomus Tertius ac Postremus*, Bologna, 1639 (29)

ALLEN, E. G. History of American Ornithology before Audubon. *Trans. Amer. Phil. Soc.* **41**: 398–591, Philadelphia, 1951

ANKER, J. *Bird Books and Bird Art*, Copenhagen, 1938

ANON. *Monk's Drawing Book*, Pepysian Library, Magdalene College, Cambridge, 14th century (15)

— *Ein Warhafftige beschreibung und urtheil von etlichen Fremden vögeln der gleichen vor nie aber jtsund in Engelandt in der Graffschafft von Licolne sind gesehen worden*, Nuremberg, 1587 (31)

— *Der 7 Vögel warhafftige Contrafectura. Innatürliche Zeyttuntungen von siben wunderbarlichen seltzamen Vögeln so in Engellandt im 1586 Jar den 27 Decembris gefangen worden . . .*, Augsburg, 1587 (32)

— *Simplicia medicamonta [sic] depicta sive icones plantarum quadrupedum avium, insectorum inservientum*, Sloane MS 4016, British Museum, 14th century (9, 10)

— *History of Birds, with a familiar Description of Each in Verse and Prose . . .*, London, 1791 (106, 107, 108, 109)

— More Ancient Treasures Excavated at Mawangtui. *China Pictorial* 11: 37–41, Peking, 1974

ARCHER, M. *Natural History Drawings in the India Office Library*, London, 1962

ARMSTRONG, E. A. *Folklore of Birds*, London, 1958

AUDUBON, J. J. *Birds of America*, London, 1831–4 (93)

BABUR, EMPEROR. *Memoirs of Babur*, illustrated by Ustad Mansur, MS, British Museum, *c.*1624 (74)

BALDNER, L. *An Exact natural Description and Delineation of the Water-Fowls . . . found in the Waters at Strassburg . . .*, MS, British Museum, 1653 (65, 66)

BARLOW, F. *Barlow's Birds and Beasts in Sixty-seven Excellent Useful Prints*, London, 1775 (57, 58)

BARNES, J. *Boke of St. Albans*, St Albans, 1486

BAUER, F. L. Original drawings, British Museum (Natural History), *c.*1802–4 (83)

BELON, P. *L'Histoire de la nature des Oyseaux . . .*, Paris, 1555 (24, 25, 48)

BERNES, JULYANA, see Barnes, J.

BEWICK, T. *Figures of British Land Birds engraved on wood*, Newcastle-on-Tyne, 1800 (112, 113, 114, 115, 116, 117)

— *Memoir of Thomas Bewick . . .*, Newcastle & London, 1862

BINNS, A. L. *Manuscript source of the Book of St. Albans*, Manchester, 1950

BLACKBURN, MRS. H. *Birds drawn from nature*, Glasgow, 1868 (141)

BOUCHARD, M. *Recueil de Cent-Trente-Trois Oiseaux des plus belles Espèces, gravés sur 87 Planches et colorés d'après Nature . . .*, Rome, 1775 (49)

BRISSON, M. J. *Ornithologie, ou méthode contenant la division des oiseaux en ordres . . .*, Paris, 1760 (81, 82)

BROWN, T. *Illustrations of the American Ornithology of Alexander Wilson and Charles Lucian Bonaparte . . .*, Edinburgh, 1831 (88)

BUFFON, G. L. L. DE. *Histoire Naturelle des Oiseaux*, Paris, 1771–6 (79, 80)

— *et al. Histoire Naturelle . . . avec la description du Cabinet du Roi*, Paris, 1749–1804

CANTIMPRÉ, THOMAS OF, see Thomas of Cantimpré

CAPUA, JOANNES DE, see Joannes de Capua

CARTWRIGHT, G. *Journal of Transactions and Events . . . on the Coast of Labrador . . .*, Newark, 1792

CASTRO, see Gomez de Castro, Alvarez

CATESBY, M. *Natural History of Carolina, Florida and the Bahama Islands . . .*, London, 1731–43 (35, 46)

CAXTON, W. *Here begynneth the book of the subtyl historyes and fables of Esop . . .*, Westminster, 1484

CHAUCER, G. 'The Assemble of Foules' from *The Boke of Fame . . . .*, London, 1526 (13)

COEITER, V. *Lectiones Gabrielis Fallopii de partibus similaribus humani corporis . . .*, Nuremberg, 1575 (22)

DESCOURTILZ, J. T. *Oiseaux brillans et remarquables du Brésil placés près des végétaux dont les fruits les nourissent* [Paris, only two copies produced], 1835 (99)

DIOSCORIDES, PEDACIUS. *Materia Medica*, 418 folios of water-colour drawings . . . copied from the *Anicia Juliana Codex*, MS, British Museum (Natural History), *c.*1458–77 (2, 3)

EDWARDS, G. *Natural history of uncommon Birds*, London, 1743–51

— *Gleanings of Natural History*, London, 1758 (77)

ELLIOT, D. G. *Monograph of the Phasianidae, or family of Pheasants*, New York, 1872 (120, 121)

English Pilot. The fourth Book. Describing the West India Navigation, from Hudson's Bay to the River Amazones, London, 1767

FABER, J. (ed.) *Animalia Mexicana descriptionibus scholiisque exposita. Thesauri rerum Medicarum Novae Hispaniae . . .*, Rome, 1628

FERNANDEZ DE OVIEDO Y VALDÉS, G. *Oviedo: de la natural hystoria de las Indias*, Toledo, 1526

FORSTER, G. Original drawings, British Museum (Natural History), 1772–5 (91, 92)

FREDERICK II. *De Arte Venandi cum Avibus*, MS Pal. Lat. 1071, Biblioteca Apostolica Vaticana (Facsimile, 1969, Graz) (5)

GERARD, J. *Herball, or generall historie of Plantes*, London, 1597

GESNER, C. *Historia Animalium*, Zurich, 1565 (26, 27)

GOMEZ DE CASTRO, ALVAREZ. (ed.) *Publica Laetitia qua dominus Joannes Martinus Silicaeus Archiepiscopus Toletanus ab Scholae Complutēsi susceptus est*, Collegium Complutense, Alċala de Henares, ?1546 (44, 45)

GOULD, J. *Icones Avium*, London, 1838 (129)

— *Monograph of the Trochilidae, or Family of Humming-Birds*, London, 1861 (94)

— *Birds of Great Britain*, London, 1863 [1862]–73 (110)

— *Supplement to the Birds of Australia*, London, 1869 (135)

— *Monograph of the Trogonidae, or Family of Trogons*, London, 1875 (98, 103)

Hardwicke's Science Gossip (ed.) J. E. Taylor, vol. 18, London, 1882

HAYES, W. *Natural History of British Birds etc. with Their Portraits Accurately drawn, and beautifully coloured from Nature*, London, 1775 (52)

HERON-ALLEN, E. *Barnacles in Nature and Myth*, Oxford, 1928

HODGSON, B. H. Collection of original drawings by Indian artists, Zoological Society of London, *c*.1820–58 (111, 140)

HODNETT, E. *English Woodcuts 1480–1535*, Oxford, 1935

HOKUSAI, see Michener, J. A.

HULTON, P. H. & QUINN, D. B. *American Drawings of John White 1577–1590*, London, 1964 (21)

HUMBOLDT, AL. DE & BONPLAND, A. *Recueil d'Observations de Zoologie et d'anatomie comparée* . . . , vol. 1, Paris, 1811 (87)

HUTCHINSON, G. E. Attitudes towards Nature in Medieval England. The Alphonso and Bird Psalters. *Isis* 65: 5–37, Washington, 1974

JACQUEMARD, S. *L'Oiseau*, Paris, 1963

JAMES, M. R. An English medieval sketch-book, no. 1916 in the Pepysian Library, Magdalene College, Cambridge. *Thirteenth Volume of the Walpole Society*, Oxford, 1924–5

JOANNES DE CAPUA. *Exemplario contra los engaños : peligros del mūdo*, Saragossa, 1531 (14)

JONES, H. Original drawings: *Alcedinae*, vol. 3, Zoological Society of London, *c*.1900 (134)

— Original drawings: *Anatidae*, vol. 5, Zoological Society of London, *c*.1890 (102)

JONSTONIUS, J. *Historiae Naturalis de Avibus*, Amsterdam, 1657 (53, 54, 56)

KONRAD VON MEGENBURG. *Buch der Natur*, Augsburg, 1481 (4)

LACÉPÈDE & CUVIER, CITOYENS. *Ménagerie du Muséum d'Histoire Naturelle ou les Animaux Vivants, peints d'après nature . . . par Maréchal et gravés par Miger*, Paris, 1801 (136)

LAISHLEY, R. *Notes and Drawings chiefly illustrating Natural Objects and Scenery in New Zealand*, MS, British Museum (Natural History), *c*.1863–83 (128)

LATHAM, J. *General Synopsis of Birds*, London, 1781–1802

LEAR, E. *Illustrations of the Family of Psittacidae or Parrots . . . drawn from life and on stone*, London, 1832 (84)

LEGUAT, F. *Voyage et avantures de F. L. . . . en deux Isles désertes des Indes Orientales . . .*, London, 1708 (60, 61)

L'OBEL, M. DE. *Plantarum seu Stirpium Historia*, Antwerp, 1576 (28)

LYSAGHT, A. M. *Joseph Banks in Newfoundland and Labrador, 1766*. London, 1971

MAGNUS, ALBERTUS, see Albertus Magnus

MAGNUS, OLAUS. *Historia de Gentibus Septentrionalibus . . .*, Rome, 1555 (36, 37, 38, 39, 40, 41, 42, 43)

— *A Compendious History of the Goths Swedes & Vandals and Other Northern Nations written by Olaus Magnus . . .*, London, 1658

MANETTI, X. *Ornithologia methodice digesta atque iconibus aeneis ad vivum illuminatis ornata*, Florence, 1767–76, (30, 85)

MANN, G. Medizinisch-naturwissenschaftlich Buch-illustration . . . , *Sber. Ges. Berförd. ges. Naturw. Marburg* 86: 3–48, Marburg, 1964

MEGENBURG, KONRAD VON, see Konrad von Megenburg

MERIAN, M. S. Original drawings, 2 vols., British Museum, undated (1)

MEYER, J. D. *Angenehmer und nützlicher Zeit-Vertreib mit Betrachtung . . .*, Nuremberg, 1748–56 (55)

MICHENER, J. A. *Hokusai Sketch Books*, Tokyo, 1960 (118, 119)

MILLER, J. F. *Various subjects of Natural History, wherein are delineated Birds, Animals and many curious Plants etc.*, London, 1776–85

NEWTON, A. *et al.* Dictionary of Birds, London, 1893–6

NISSEN, C. *Illustrierten Vogelbücher Geschichte und Bibliographie*, Stuttgart, 1953

— *Herbals of five centuries*, Zurich, 1958

NOZEMAN, C. *Nederlandsche Vogelen . . .*, Amsterdam, 1770–1829 (67, 97)

OLINA, G. P. *Uccelliera overo discorso della natura e proprieta di diversi uccelli . . .*, Rome, 1622 (69, 70, 71, 72)

OVIEDO, see Fernandez de Oviedo y Valdés, G.

PALLAS, P. S. *Spicilegia Zoologica*, Berlin, 1769 (104, 105)

PARKINSON, S. Original drawings. British Museum, 1767, (63)

PENNANT, T. *British Zoology*, London & Chester, 1766; 3rd ed. 1768

— *Zoologica Britannica tabulis aeneis CXXXII illustrata*, Augsburg, 1771 (101)

— *Arctic Zoology*, London, 1784–7 (89, 90)

— *Indian Zoology*, 2nd ed., London, 1790

PLANTIN, C. *Icones Stirpium seu Plantarum tam exoticarum quam indigenarum . . .*, Antwerp, 1591 (28)

PLINIUS SECUNDUS, C. *Historie of the World . . .*, translated by Philemon Holland, London, 1634

RAPER, G. Original drawings. British Museum (Natural History) *c*.1787 (73, 76)

READ, B. Chinese Materia Medica VI, Avian Drugs, *Peking Nat. Hist. Bull.* 6: 1–112, 1931–2

READE, B. *Edward Lear's Parrots*, London, 1949

REEVES, J. Original drawings by Chinese artists. British Museum (Natural History), early 19th century (78)

ROLLER, D. H. D. (ed.) *Perspectives in the History of Science and Technology*, Oklahoma, 1971

ROTHSCHILD, W. Monograph of the genus *Casuarius*. *Trans. Zoo. Soc. London* 15: 109–48, 1901 (137)

RYDER, A. W. *Panchatantra. Translated from the Sanskrit . . .*, Chicago, 1925

SCHELLER, R. W. *Survey of Medieval Model Books*, Haarlem, 1963

SELBY, P. J. *Illustrations of British Ornithology*, Edinburgh & London, 1821 (123)

— & JARDINE, W. *Naturalist's Library*, vols. 9, 15, Edinburgh & London, 1835, 1836

SHARPE, R. BOWDLER. *Monograph of the Paradiseidae or Birds of Paradise and Ptilonothynicidae or Bower Birds*, London, 1891–8 (138, 139)

SHAW, G. *Cimelia Physica*, London, 1796 (100)

SHERBORNE MISSAL. MS, Library of the Duke of Northumberland, c.1396–1407 (7, 8)

SONNERAT, P. *Voyage à la Nouvelle Guinée*, Paris, 1776, (95)

STUBBS, G. *Comparative Anatomical exposition of the structure of the Human Body with that of a Tiger and Common Fowl*, London, 1804–6 (86)

SUSEMIHL, J. C. *Abbildungen aus dem Thierreiche . . . Ornithologie*, Darmstadt, 1821–6 (132, 133)

TATON, R. (ed.) *Beginnings of Modern Science from 1450 to 1800*, London, 1964

TERRACE, E. L. B. *Egyptian Paintings of the Middle Kingdom*, London, 1968

THOMAS OF CANTIMPRÉ. *De natura rerum*, MS, 1228–44, see Konrad of Megenburg

THOMPSON, D'ARCY W. *Glossary of Greek Birds*, Oxford, 1895

THOMSON, A. LANDSBOROUGH. *New Dictionary of Birds*, London & Edinburgh, 1964

TUPPO, FRANCESCO DEL. *Libistici Fabulatores Esopi Vita Feliciter Incipit*, Naples, 1485 (16, 17, 18)

TURNER, W. *Avium precipuarum quarum apud Plinium et Aristotelem Mentio est . . .* , Cologne, 1544

TYSON, E. *Orang-Outang, or The Anatomy of a Pigmie compared with that of a Monkey, an Ape, and a Man*, London, 1699

VALENTIJN, F. *Omstandig Verhaal van de Geschiedenissen . . . in Amboina*, Amsterdam, 1724–6 (75)

VIEILLOT, L. J. P. *Histoire Naturelle des Oiseaux de l'Amérique Septentrionale . . .* , Paris, 1807 (127)

WALLACE, A. R. *Malay Archipelago: the land of the Orang-Utan and the Bird of Paradise. A narrative of travels with studies of man and nature*, London, 1869 (130, 131)

WEBB-SMITH, C. *Birds, Flowers and Scenery of the Cape of Good Hope*, MS, Balfour Library, Zoology Department, University of Cambridge, 1839–59 (125)

— & D'OYLY, C. *Indian Birds and Scenery*, MS, Balfour Library, Zoology Department, University of Cambridge, c.1829–59 (126)

WELLESLEY, R. C. Collection of original drawings by Indian artists, India Office Library, London, c.1797–1802 (59, 122)

WILLUGHBY, F. *Ornithologiae Libri Tres: in quibus Aves omnes hactenus cognitae in Methodum Naturis suis convenientem redactae, accurate describuntur . . .* , London, 1676 (62, 64)

WOLF, J. Original drawings, *Aves*, vol. 5, Zoological Society of London, c.1840–90 (124)

WORM, O. *Museum Wormianum, seu Historia rerum rariorum . . .* , Leyden, 1655 (68, 96)

Index

Index of Birds

Index of Names